need to know...

Golf

All the kit, techniques and inspiration
you need to get into the game

First published in 2004 by
Collins, an imprint of
HarperCollins*Publishers*
77-85 Fulham Palace Road
Hammersmith, London W6 8JB

The Collins website address is:
www.collins.co.uk

Collins is a registered trademark of HarperCollins Publishers Limited.

08 07 06 05 04
6 5 4 3 2 1

© HarperCollins*Publishers*, 2004

A catalogue record for this book is available from the British Library

Created by: SP Creative Design
Editor: Heather Thomas
Designer: Rolando Ugolini
Photographer: Rolando Ugolini
Cover design: Cook Design
Front cover photograph: © Lori Adamski Peek/Getty Images
Back cover photographs: Rolando Ugolini

ISBN 0 00 718037 3

Colour reproduction by Colourscan, Singapore
Printed and bound by Printing Express Ltd, Hong Kong

contents

Introduction

With its wonderful flexibility and equitable handicap system, golf is unique in enabling players of all ages and abilities to enjoy the game and play together. You can set aside four hours to play a full 18 holes either against yourself or with one, two or three companions, or, if you cannot afford the time, you may just play nine holes.

Why is golf so popular?

People enjoy playing golf for a variety of reasons and it has become one of the fastest growing and most popular sports. Its benefits include:

- It exercises your body and is good for your health. During a round, you will walk about four miles in the fresh air in a beautiful environment.
- It enables you to meet new people and play with your friends. You can engage in business or just be sociable during a round or afterwards in the club house on the nineteenth tee.
- It can satisfy our competitive instincts as it can be played in many different formats, ranging from a casual two-ball to a formal tournament.
- Almost anywhere you travel, on business or pleasure, all over the world, you can find a course and enjoy playing a round of golf.
- Many golfers make useful business introductions out on the course. The very nature of the game makes it ideal for hospitality and entertaining.

Golf is never boring

Even your home course will always present you with new challenges and infinite variations every time you play. The weather and course conditions will change according to the season, and there may be unfamiliar hazards to overcome. Your own technical ability and performance will vary, too. On good days, you will be delighted with your repertoire of shots and low scores, whereas on others you will despair of your inability to recover well from lurking bunkers, sand traps, water hazards, thick rough, poor lies and inconveniently placed trees.

Even though there will be a few odd days when hitting a golf ball is frustratingly difficult, there will also be glorious times when your game flows and the hitting is easy. This book will give you all the basic information you need when you are starting out in golf, helping you to master the technical fundamentals, learn the value of practice and develop a consistent approach and the right mental attitude so that you can enjoy this marvellous game.

equipment

for golf

There is a massive amount of choice when it comes to golf equipment and clothing. Trying to select the right set of golf clubs for your physique and ability can be very confusing, especially as an enormous range is now available, but it is not necessary to spend a fortune. Ask your local golf professional to advise on which clubs will suit you best.

Choosing golf clubs

This is one of the most important decisions and expensive purchases that you will make so it is important to get it right. Your PGA professional will guide you in selecting equipment.

Half or full set?

If you still don't know whether golf is going to be the right game for you, you may consider investing in a used half set which is adequate for a beginner, provided that the clubs are suitable for your height and build. However, be on your guard and beware of what may appear to be a terrific bargain but which will have no value at all if it does not suit you and your individual needs!

All golf clubs appear to be much the same to most beginners, but there are some important variations in their construction which you must consider, whether you want to buy a full set, a half set or just a specific club to start you off.

▲ Traditional wood laminate heads were made from wooden strips glued together. Now rare, they have been overtaken by metal heads.

◀ Most modern clubs have metal heads with either carbon or steel shafts. You can also buy cheaper alloys at the lower end of the market. High-tech carbon heads are acknowledged to be the best you can buy.

What to look for

Golfers' physical builds differ considerably and thus we require different clubs. Being fitted correctly for your golf clubs is like choosing well-fitting clothes. You need to take into account your height, arm and leg length, body length, hand size, strength and natural rhythm as these will influence the way you stand and swing the club and therefore the type of club you should use.

Things to consider

When considering which clubs to buy, you should take the following factors into account: lie of the club, loft and shaft length, grip thickness, weight distribution and club head design, shaft flexibility and overall weight and swing weight.

Lie of the club

This is the angle between the sole of the club head and the shaft. It is important in iron clubs where you should take a divot. If the lie is not right, the heel or toe of the club will dig into the ground, causing the club head to twist at impact. Throughout a set of irons the lie angle will vary according to the graduating length of the shaft.

▲ These 5 iron clubs are available in flat, standard and upright lie options. Notice how the soles of all three clubs are sitting flat on the ground.

Most irons are designed with a slightly curved sole so that when you are addressing the ball, the heel and toe cannot both touch the ground. It is preferable to have the toe just off the ground with the sole sitting between the heel and the centre of the club. This is because the force of the swing causes the shaft to bow outwards slightly during the return swing.

Your height and your arm length will determine whether you will need standard lie clubs. If you are tall and your fingertips are more than 72 cm (29 in) from the ground when you are standing erect, your clubs should be more upright than standard. If your fingertip to ground measurement is less than 70 cm (27 in), you will need flatter lie clubs.

If you fall into either category, you must adopt the correct posture in your set up to establish the necessary degree of alteration from standard.

Loft and shaft lengths

Golf clubs fall into two groups: woods and irons. Woods have come a long way since their original wooden shafts and are now constructed from stainless steel, graphite and even titanium. Steel shafts are popular as they are accurate and less expensive, but lightweight graphite and titanium add weight to the club head to help you create higher, more powerful shots which travel further.

The loft and shaft length vary with each club. From the driver to the pitching wedge, the loft angle increases from 10 degrees to a backward slant of 50 degrees. As loft increases by increments of four degrees, the shaft length decreases by 125 mm (¹/₂ in) per club in each of the groups.

▲ The shaft length varies according to the club you are using and this affects the way in which you set up and position the ball.

◄ The loft of a club, as is indicated here by the lines, is 15 degrees in the case of this No. 3 wood.

WHICH LOFT IS RIGHT FOR YOU?

Desired loft on modern metal drivers

Children up to 12 years	15 degrees of loft
Children 12-14 years	13 degrees of loft
Boys 14-16 years	11 degrees of loft
Girls 14-16 years	12 degrees of loft
Men below 8 handicap*	8-10 degrees of loft
Women below 8 handicap*	10-11 degrees of loft
Men 8-20 handicap*	10-12 degrees of loft
Women 8-20 handicap*	11-12 degrees of loft
Men above 20 handicap	13-15 degrees of loft
Women above 20 handicap	13-15 degrees of loft

*Add one degree if aged over 50 and two degrees if over 60.

Woods loft table
(in degrees)

Club	Pro	Men	Women
No 1	10°	12°	12°
No 2	12°	14°	14°
No 3	14°	16°	16°
No 4	19°	20°	20°
No 5	23°	24°	25°

Club head design

Most amateur golfers will hit better shots with a perimeter weighted club head. Beginners and high handicappers are not likely to strike the ball right in the centre of the club face all the time so they can benefit from a club whose weight is distributed around the perimeter of the head. This has the effect of making the sweet spot bigger and will allow you to get away with an off-centre hit better than if you used a blade club.

- **Blade clubs** are more classic with clean lines as opposed to the chunky rounded edges of most perimeter weighted clubs. They are beloved of purists, low-handicappers and professionals, who have a better technique and strike the ball in the centre of the club most of the time.

- **Iron club heads** are manufactured in two ways – cast or forged – and each has its own merits. As a learner, it is better to start off with a cast club because the steel is harder and more durable and requires less careful maintenance. The more advanced player may benefit from forged clubs because these are made of a mild steel which gives a softer feel and more controlled ball flight, but they will dent and mark more easily, especially if used on a stony course.

▲ Three distinctly different designs of iron heads. From the top: a forged blade; a forged heel and toe weighted club; and a cast heel and toe weighted club (harder steel).

Irons loft table
(in degrees)

Club	Men	Ladies
No 2	19°	—
No 3	23°	24°
No 4	27°	28°
No 5	31°	32°
No 6	35°	36°
No 7	39°	40°
No 8	43°	44°
No 9	47°	48°

Pro/tournament irons are usually one degree less than mens' irons.

▲ Carbon head drivers are expensive but incorporate modern golf technology.

▲ Metal head drivers usually have an enlarged sweet spot – the area of ideal contact on the club face.

Shaft flexibility

It is vital that your clubs have the correct shaft flex for you or they will harm your swing and lead to mishits. The flexes available are: ladies', flexible mens', regular, stiff and extra stiff. Manufacturers have their own ways of measuring and grading shafts. Therefore one company's regular shaft may equate to a stiff one in another range.

The shaft is the powerhouse of the golf club, transferring the power of your swing to the club head. Your physical strength, hand action and speed of swing will determine which flex you need. A slow swing is better suited to more flexible shafts, but if you are strong with a fast swing, a stiffer shaft will help you. If an older player with a slow swing uses too stiff a shaft, the ball may go straight but will lack distance. A strong swinger using a very flexible shaft may hit the ball a long way but without any control over direction.

Choosing the right shaft flex

Aim for the correct balance between distance and accuracy. As a learner, it may be too early to know whether you tend to hit the ball high or low but you should understand how shaft flex affects the ball flight. The shaft can be made to bend most at a low flex point, i.e. nearer the club head, which will help you hit the ball higher. Alternatively, a high flex point, which is nearer to the grip of the club, will tend to produce a lower ball flight. Most learners are better with a low flex point because it encourages them to get the ball airborne.

▲ Older golfers may not have the physical strength and flexibility of younger players. If you are a senior with a slow swing, you should play with clubs with more flexible shafts.

Overall weight

The overall weight of the club is the dead weight, or total weight, of all the components. The swing weight is the balance between the club head weight related to the weight of the grip and shaft. This is the measurement of the club head's weight which you feel when you swing the club.

Swing weights

These are measured in scales from A to D and within each letter from 0–9 (lightest to heaviest). Ignore the A and B scales as they are ultra light. The standard range for ladies is between C4–C7; and for men between D0–D2. A set of clubs should be matched for swing weight.

Your choice is likely to be influenced more by the speed of your swing than physical strength. Even top pros use clubs of different swing weights although they may be of a similar height and build. This is usually due to the speed of their swing, some being slower or brisker than others. A naturally fast swing needs the extra club head weight or it is likely to become just too fast.

The weight of the club head will influence how the shaft flexes. A standard, regular shaft will flex more with a heavy club head at the end of it than a light one. Also, the length of the shaft

Club anatomy

- **Club face:** The total area of the club head where the ball should be struck.
- **Sweet spot:** The part of the club face at which, when a ball is struck correctly, the best shot is produced.
- **Hosel:** This is the part of the club head where the shaft enters the head.
- **Shank** (or heel): The part of the club head which is nearest to the hosel.
- **Toe:** The part of the club head furthest away from the hosel.
- **Sole:** This is the underneath of the club head which rests on the ground.

◀ A range of shafts (from left to right): flex twist carbon, boron tipped carbon, a normal carbon shaft, and a lightweight steel shaft.

Choosing the swing weight

Here are some basic guidelines to help you choose the right swing weight for you and your game:

- C0–C5: Less strong lady player.
- C5–C8: Good lady player to older man.
- D0: Average man player.
- D2: Good man player.

influences the swing weight, so if you are short and require a shorter than standard shaft it will make the swing weight lighter unless other adjustments are made; self-adhesive lead tape is available for this purpose.

As you have probably realized by now, all these factors are linked and affect each other. Whilst it is not essential to have custom-fitted clubs when you are starting out in golf, it is essential to get the lie, grip thickness and shaft flex correct right at the very beginning. Even if you decide on one or two clubs or a second-hand set, ask your pro to advise you on what best suits your build and natural method.

▶ Club head size is more important in drivers than most other clubs. From left to right: large, mid-size and normal metal heads.

Pitching and sand wedges

If you decide to start with a half set of clubs you will probably have either a pitching wedge or a sand wedge but not both. However, it is worth noting the difference in design of these two clubs and the purposes they are required to perform.

- **The pitching wedge** has a flat, narrow sole with a straight leading edge, encouraging a crisp contact with the ball even from a hard, bare lie.
- **The sand wedge** sole is heavier and more rounded, and the back edge of the sole is lower than the front leading edge. This is to help the club bounce through the sand and not dig in too

◄ To blast your way out of bunkers, you will need to invest in a sand wedge which will travel through the sand easily and pop the ball up back on to the course.

deeply, which a pitching wedge tends to do. The sand wedge is the heaviest club head in a set, and it encourages the club to keep on moving through the sand and the ball.

Although its name implies that it is used mainly in bunkers, the sand wedge may also be used from grass, but you should take care as you will need some soft grass underneath the ball. From a hard, bare lie, it is not advisable to use this club because its sole will tend to bounce and you would then catch the ball very thin.

▼ This shows the difference between a sand wedge and a pitching wedge. Notice the space under the front edge of the sand wedge (left). It sits on the flange at the back of the sole whereas the pitching wedge has a flat sole to allow the leading front edge to be on the ground.

▲ This shows two different lie angles for putters. Both soles are flat to the ground but note the shaft angles. They influence the distance you stand from the ball.

▲ These three putter heads show varying degrees of offset, which is designed to position your hands forward of the striking face. From the left: no offset; 1/4 inch offset; and 1/2 inch offset.

Putters

Choosing the right putter is an extremely personal decision as there are so many designs available, ranging from traditional shapes to some ultra modern ones. There are no simple rules; you just have to find the one that works best for you. If you can get the ball in the hole and are confident with any design of putter, then use it.

This is the golf club you will use most in a round and is therefore perhaps the most important one in your bag. Most established golfers have two or three spare putters because inevitably the old faithful will misbehave occasionally and confidence will fade; this is the time for a change, even for a short period. Then when you return to your favourite again, it will feel a lot better.

Many top professionals have used dozens of different putters during their careers although some have stuck to one in the belief that if it has performed well in the past it cannot be the fault of the putter if they sometimes miss putts.

Putter shaft lengths

These vary from 80 cm (32 in) to 90 cm (36 in), so shaft length is worth considering if you happen to be tall or short. However, a shorter shaft will make the head weight feel lighter, and a longer shaft increases the feel of the head weight. It is also a good idea to choose a putter with a lie angle that allows you to keep the sole flat, and you should stand with your eye line over the ball.

A recent trend is the introduction of the very long-shafted putter which is held with the top of the grip against either your chin or chest, and the hands split by up to 45 cm (18 in). Although these putters have been the saviour of quite a number of Tour players, they are not recommend for beginners. It is worth trying this 'broom handle' length putter only if you have persevered with a standard length and really struggled.

Grip thickness

This will be determined by the size of your hands and length of your fingers. Thus ladies' grips are the thinnest, whereas specially manufactured Jumbo grips are the thickest ones.

The Jumbo grip is designed for people with large hands but is also beneficial for the older player who suffers from arthritis and finds it difficult to close their fingers. Your club grip can be packed to the correct thickness for you so seek the advice of your teaching professional.

Aim to have the fingers of your left hand just touching the fleshy part of your thumb joint when they are closed around the grip. The right hand should then be able to hold the grip in the fingers and fall with the fleshy part of the right thumb joint on top of the left thumb.

Too thin a grip will cause the fingertips to dig into the palm of your hand, whereas too thick a grip will not allow your fingers to close properly around it. Make sure that the grip of your putter is right for you.

▲ When the golf club grip is the correct thickness, this is the hold position that you should obtain with your hands comfortably around it.

▲ If the club grip is too thin, the left hand will be in a poor position and your fingers will be sticking into the flesh of your hands.

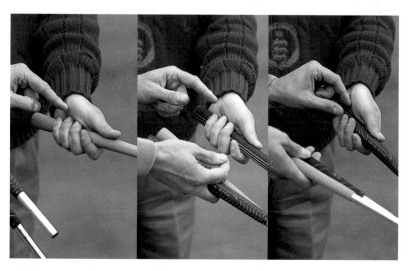

▲ Find the correct grip thickness: the finger should just meet the fleshy part of the thumb joint (centre). The thumb joint overlapping the fingers (left) or a space (right) is unsuitable.

Other equipment

In addition to a set of golf clubs, you will need a bag to carry them in and a few other items of specialist equipment plus the right clothing and shoes for venturing out on to the course. Here's some useful information to help you choose.

▲ You can use specially designed head covers to protect your woods. If you are playing in a match you are allowed to carry a maximum of 14 clubs.

▲ You can either opt for a lightweight carrying bag and fewer clubs or a hand-pulled trolley for a heavier bag with a full set of clubs.

Bags

You must decide first whether you want to use a trolley or carry your clubs before you select a bag. If you wish to use a trolley, particularly an electric one, then you can opt for a larger bag, which will allow more storage space for your clubs and clothing. Many beginners prefer to use a lightweight carrying bag, which is more sensible if you are not planning to start off with a full set of clubs.

For a full set, the base of the bag needs to be large enough for all the grips to fit without jamming. This makes it difficult to remove each club and can damage the grips. Nowadays, many bags have dividers which continue down halfway or to the base, giving you easier access to your clubs. Golf bags may be made of lightweight nylon, PVC or even leather. This will influence the price, leather being the most expensive. During the damp winter months, when the ground is often wet with dew, you may need a bag stand on your carrybag in order to protect the base.

Trolleys

These fall into two categories: hand pulled or electric motorized for less strong players. Of the pull types, there are fold-up ones with the bag attached and others where you remove the bag. The larger the bag, the stronger the trolley must be. A full golf bag plus trolley is potentially quite heavy and many trolley manufacturers use lightweight alloys to compensate for this.

Golf balls

These can be split into two distinct groups:

- Two-piece, solid core.
- Wound, three-piece construction.

Two-piece balls are preferable for the beginner because they are very durable and have a lower spin rate which maximizes the roll distance and minimizes side spin, which causes hooked or sliced shots. However, they will not stop so quickly on the green.

Wound balls are available with two types of cover: surlyn (man-made) or natural balata. A wound balata ball is the ultimate performance ball for many low-handicappers but not for the average player. Surlyn wound balls offer control and feel characteristics that are similar to those of a balata ball but are also much more durable.

Compression balls

Most wound balls are now available in two compression options – 90 or 100 – which are a measurement of a golf ball's resistance to impact force. A lower compression golf ball will flatten against the club face to a greater degree than a higher compression ball when it is subjected to the same impact. A player who generates a lot of club head speed will favour the 100 compression ball, feeling that the 90 compression ball will be too soft at impact.

MUST KNOW

Effects of temperature

Bear in mind when you are playing out on the course in different conditions that all golf balls are affected considerably by temperature. A warm ball will be more springy and will therefore compress more easily and travel further than a cold ball, which feels harder and is less able to compress. Therefore if you are playing in an important competition, take the local temperature into account when you are judging distance and planning your shots.

▲ Always buy reasonable quality golf balls but, as a beginner, it is not worth you investing in the ultimate performance balls used by the Tour pros as you will not be skillful enough to take advantage of them and you may lose a lot around the course during a round.

Caring for your clubs

To ensure that your set of golf clubs stays looking good and working for you with maximum efficiency, you should take care of them, cleaning them each time you play.

The golden rules

- Always wipe any dirt off the face of the club with a towel after each shot.
- Make sure you wipe the ball clean before teeing off on each hole. Carry a towel in your bag.
- Occasionally you should use a groove scraping tool and brush to remove any dirt from the club face grooves.
- Always keep head covers on your woods, even if they are of metal construction. Iron covers are a good idea for graphite shaft irons.
- Do not leave your clubs wet after play – you should always dry them with a towel.

Any dirt on the ball or the club face will result in an abrasive action on both surfaces at impact and could cause an inconsistent flight of the ball. This applies especially to your wooden clubs, even if they are of metal construction.

▲ Always protect your woods with head covers even if they are made of metal.

▲ Clean the club face with a stiff brush (top) and then use a tee to remove any dirt from the grooves (above).

◀ You can clean your club heads with their covers if you do not have a towel.

Clothing

You should wear comfortable clothes which to move without restriction. To play well, you need to look and feel comfortable. Certain standards of dress are expected at most golf clubs.

Waterproof clothing

Golf is often played in wet conditions and you will need a waterproof suit made of a breathable material, such as Goretex, or at least a lightweight waterproof jacket for emergencies that you can tuck into a pocket of your golf bag.

▲ You can wear a leather or synthetic glove to produce adhesion at the top of the backswing. Make sure that the glove is comfortable and fits you correctly.

Shoes

You walk at least four miles during an average round so it is important to have comfortable shoes which you can wear, no matter what the weather. Buy a breathable waterproof shoe with studs which you can wear all the year round or keep a leather pair for dry weather and another waterproof pair for wet conditions. Metal spikes are fitted to most golf shoes, but rubber studs are also very comfortable, especially when the ground is hard; don't wear if the ground is soft.

Gloves

Most golfers wear a glove on the upper hand: the left hand for a right-handed player. It helps to give adhesion, especially at the top of the backswing and at impact in the event of a mishit.

● Leather gloves are traditional and give the most sensitive feel in dry conditions.

● Synthetic gloves not only look and feel like leather but they also perform very well, cost less, last longer and are good in wet conditions.

● All weather gloves were originally gloves that were not very good in dry conditions. However, with the recent improvements made to synthetic materials, they now perform well when dry or wet.

want to know more?

Take it to the next level...

Go to...
▶ **Taking lessons** – page 26
▶ **The set up** – page 36
▶ **The swing** – page 45

Other sources
▶ **Specialist suppliers and fitters**
  for custom-fitted clubs
▶ **Internet sources**
  buy discounted equipment on line
▶ **Golf pro shops – try your local club**
  can advise on club selection
▶ **Golf magazines**
  advertisements for equipment
▶ **Sports retailers and stores**
  for golf clothing

starting to

play golf

As a beginner, you cannot just go out on to the course and start playing. Golf is a technical game and you need to learn the basic skills and practise them before you can expect to play the game. So enrol with your local golf professional for a course of lessons and spend time practising not only out on the driving range or practice ground but also at home.

Taking lessons

Before you rush straight to the course and expect to be able to play the game, take some time to learn the correct basic skills on a driving range or practice ground with a golf pro.

Seek out a pro

Many beginners have tried playing a few rounds of golf with a friend, then realized that golf is not as easy as they thought. When they finally seek the services of a golf professional, many faults have to be undone before the correct fundamentals of golfing technique can be introduced.

▼ You can't learn all you need to know about playing golf from a book, and it is always best to take lessons from your local professional.

Choose your teacher carefully and check that they are prepared to teach you from scratch. Some professionals specialize in specific areas of the game and may not teach beginners. Try to find one who inspires you with confidence and with whom you can establish a rapport. Don't be afraid to ask for advice on all aspects of the game.

What sort of lessons?

When you book your lessons, try to get your first ones closely grouped – perhaps one or two per week to help you build a consistent set up and basic swing so you hit the ball with a degree of reliability before you attempt playing a round of golf. Also, practise as much as you can between lessons to train your golf muscles.

Learning a good swing early on is just as important an investment as the equipment you buy, so allocate a large percentage of your financial outlay on golf tuition and, if necessary, economize on your clubs. Do not hunt out the cheapest lessons – they will not be very good.

▲ As well as taking lessons from a qualified golf pro, you can benefit from watching instructional videos and DVDs, and even from asking a friend to film your swing and then analyzing it as you watch it on the screen.

Group tuition

This is an inexpensive way of getting started. Many pros run evening classes but you will share the teacher with other people. If you can afford it, a one-to-one relationship or learning in a smaller group will give you the best chance to progress.

Be patient

Golf cannot be learned in a weekend, and as long as you play you can still improve if you are reasonably fit. It is worth asking your pro to check out your game even after you have developed a sound swing to avoid slipping back into bad habits. There is no limit to the number of lessons you can take, whatever your ability and experience. Even top pros continue to take lessons from their favourite golfing gurus.

MUST KNOW

Warm up

It is a good idea to get into a routine of warming up before you play, especially on a cold wintry day when a small strain could seriously affect your swing. Turn to page 136 for a basic warm-up routine and fitness exercises.

Practice

Regular practice will tell the brain as accurately as possible how to organize the movements of the body. To practise constructively you must have the right thoughts in your mind.

Set yourself goals

Golf is a target game, so practice should always include targets. Make your practice as similar as possible to the real thing, especially the swing. Your aim and alignment are always crucial factors; if they are not correct, then your swing will compensate with faults. Check that your thoughts and reality correspond by placing some clubs on the ground to check your feet, club face and ball positions.

Once you have a target and aim in mind, you should try to visualize the shot you are practising. For instance, imagine the flight that the ball will take. How high is the flight? Where will the ball land and how much roll will it have? Set yourself some competitive goals, such as hitting seven out of ten bunker shots on to the green, or maybe eight out of ten drives between two target trees. Play a number of chips and putts from different positions around the green and see how many times you can get down in two.

▲ You may find it useful in practice when setting up for a shot to lay some clubs on the ground through which to swing at your target.

28

MUST KNOW

Be positive
Just aimlessly hitting balls on the practice ground or the driving range is nothing more than mere physical exercise; it will not improve your game and may do damage.

Vary your shots

Never practise hitting the ball flat out with any club. To promote control and feel, practise half- and three-quarter shots, then hit two different lofted clubs the same distance. You will soon realize the distance that can be achieved with little effort. Do not always practise with the same clubs; introduce lots of variation. After a lesson, you may need to change a position or movement in the swing; it may be more effective not to make a full swing but to isolate the defect and repeat the correct move until it blends naturally into the whole swing.

At-home practice drills

There are several routines that you can practise at home. In the early stages of learning, these are just as good as hitting the ball although you do need to learn some ball contact and feel as well. Here are some drills for you to try out yourself.

Putting track drill

Lay a piece of 10 x 5 cm (4 x 2 in) timber flat on the ground. Position the heel of your putter so that it is touching and running along the edge of the wood to give the feeling for the straight section of a correct putting stroke. The length of stroke used would not propel the ball more than about 15 feet on an average-speed surface. **Note**: Two club shafts may also be used (as shown right) to give a parallel lines impression to aid the ingraining of a good putting stroke.

One-arm swing

In order to strengthen and gain control, use your left arm only to swing the club, placing your right arm behind your back and swinging halfway back and through. Keep your eyes focused on the spot where the ball would be. If you feel that the club is too heavy then move down the grip two or three inches.

▲ The putting track drill is being performed here with two parallel club shafts. Use it to practise your pendulum putting swing (see page 104).

◀ This practice drill will help you to strengthen your left arm, which tends to be weaker in right-handed people, and gain control.

▲ Chip some airballs into a
target such as a bucket lid.
Use a mat if necessary to
protect your grass.

Door mat drill

If you have a well-tended lawn from which you do
not want to remove any divots, just place your
back door mat (coconut type) on some grass or
a hard surface outside. You need an object to
represent the ball – a piece of tape, a painted
mark or some golf tees at which to aim – so that
when you swing down to the mat you can see
that your club head is returning consistently to the
correct point at the bottom of the swing.

Club head control drill

Keep a club at home in a convenient place to
encourage you to pick it up frequently. This allows
you to practise your grip and become more
familiar with the club as an extension of you. Grip
the club and hold the head up at around shoulder
height with no bend at your hips. Then trace your
name in large letters in the air. Don't move your
body or arms, but do this by flexing your hands
and wrists up and down and back and forth, all
the time looking at the club head. Remember
that your hands are the direct link with the club
head good golf begins with a good grip.

▼ This drill will help you to develop better control of your
hands as well as the club head. When you are gripping the
club, think of it as an extension of your arms and hands.

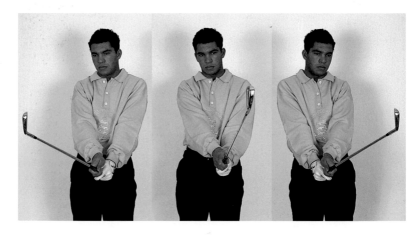

STARTING TO PLAY GOLF

Head against wall drill

Your aim is to feel your head staying steady whilst your body turns around it. Adopt your normal set up with your head lightly touching a wall. Take your normal golf grip, without a club, your right index finger approximately 7 cm (3 in) from the wall, your feet 22 cm (9 in) away. When you swing, note the arc your hands make in relation to the wall, moving away from the wall on both sides, then returning close to it in the middle section of the swing.

Cross hands drill

Taking your normal set-up position, cross your extended arms, with the back of your right hand over and against the back of your left. Swing the arms away from the target, turning your body, resisting with the back of your left hand until you reach the top of the backswing. Hold for a few seconds. From the set-up position, reverse your hands, left over and against the right this time. Counter the swing towards the target by resisting with the back of your right hand and hold the followthrough position for a few seconds. Repeat, concentrating on target side leadership and maintaining consistent balance.

▲ The hands are now reversed right over left. The follow through movement is made with resistance from the back of the left hand, holding for a few seconds.

▲ Start with the left wrist crossed over the right and the backs of the hands touching. Make a normal backswing turn, forcibly resisting with the back of the right hand.

STARTING TO PLAY GOLF

31

▲ Place your hands about 30 cm (12 in) apart, and keep the centre part of the rolled towel taut throughout. There should be good arm rotation which will help golfers who slice to use the correct golf grip.

▼ Try swinging your arms initially without a golf club. Set up as though you are going to hit a ball and then swing your arms to and fro.

Towel drill

Hold the centre part of the towel rolled up with your left hand, palm facing down, and your right hand, palm facing up, 30 cm (12 in) apart. Then adopt your normal stance and posture and swing the towel around your body as if it were a golf club, keeping the towel taut throughout. You should be aware of the rotation of your hands and forearms within the swing. Repeat the exercise with continuous movements. Modify the exercise by releasing your right hand just as the forward swing begins, then continuing with the left hand and arm to fling the towel forcefully out towards the target for a high finish.

Elephant's trunk drill

As a beginner, you may find it easier initially to create a swinging movement without a golf club in your hand. Assume your correct stance and posture, extending your hands in a near-vertical plane and clapping your hands together. Swing your extended arms back and through, keeping in your mind a mental picture of both the arms swinging together as one, and the swing being initiated from your shoulders. You should use this exercise only at waist height, keeping both your arms fully extended throughout.

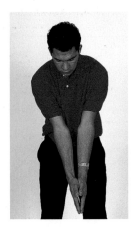

Club support drills

Take your correct stance and place the palm of your left hand on top of the club shaft which should be vertical. Start with your right hand in a normal grip position but with the fingers pointed downwards so that the palm of your hand faces your imaginary target and your right elbow points inwards towards your right hip.

Turn your body away to make a backswing, letting your right wrist hinge back and keeping your left arm and the club still. Return to the impact position with your hips turned to face the target and your right palm facing the target with some hinge at the wrist retained. Be aware of your right shoulder being lower than your left.

Reverse the exercise and repeat with your right hand placed on top of the club, swinging your left arm back and pulling through with left-side force to a high finishing position. Repeat both these exercises several times.

▲ Start with the palm of the left hand resting on top of the club shaft, then swing the right arm back and return it to a simulated impact position. Your hips should start to turn to face the target with your right palm slightly downwards.

▲ Repeat the exercise with your right hand on top of the club. Swing your left hand back to simulate the follow through.

want to know more?

Take it to the next level...

Go to...
- ▶ **Warm-up exercises** – page 136
- ▶ **Golf fitness** – page 138
- ▶ **Building a swing** – page 35

Other sources
- ▶ **Your local golf professional**
  for a course of lessons
- ▶ **Videos and DVDs**
  for easy-to-follow basic instruction
- ▶ **Internet**
  interactive CD-ROMs
- ▶ **Magazines**
  for instructional articles
- ▶ **Publications**
  visit www.collins.co.uk for Collins golf books

building a

good swing

You need to appreciate what it takes in order to build a good, consistent golf swing. This chapter focuses on the different key parts of the set up and swing. If you practise each part in the correct order, you will build a swing of which you can be proud. You must also learn to modify your set up when you use different irons and woods.

The set up

Golf is a game of repetition. It demands a good routine to bring about the consistency of shots required to keep your scores low out on the course, and that routine starts with the set up, the foundation of a sound, rhythmic swing.

Five parts of the set up

If your set up is good, all the subsequent actions in the swing are more likely to be simple and successful. It is all too easy to rush through this first part and gallop on to what is often seen as the business end of golf – hitting the ball. Do not allow yourself to fall into this trap.

The set up consists of all the things you must do before you take a swing. It can be separated into five distinct parts in the order in which they occur:

- **Aim**: align your club to the target.
- **Grip**: place your hands on the club.
- **Ball position**: position your body in relation to the ball.
- **Body alignment**: align your body to the target.
- **Posture**: position your body for the shot.

As you deal with all the parts of the set up highlighted above, it is very important to keep working around your natural body movements, and you will see reference to this throughout the swing-building process in this chapter.

▲ A good set up should become an intrinsic part of your routine when you are preparing to take a shot. If done correctly, you give yourself a better chance of producing a successful stroke and avoiding the most common swing faults.

MUST KNOW

Train your body and mind

Learning to play golf is essentially a training process, not as physically demanding as soccer or tennis, but as skilled as playing a musical instrument. It takes time to train your mind to control your muscles in a new way. Knowing how to move is not enough – to be consistent and improve your scores you must practise the basic golf moves and exercises until they are ingrained and you can repeat them without thinking about what you are doing, automatically and instinctively.

Aim

The part of the club you aim with is the bottom front edge, called the 'leading edge'. You must establish a right-angled (90 degrees) relationship between the edge and your target line in order to aim the club correctly. To do this, prepare your shot in the following way every time. This is the beginning of your routine.

Ball-to-target-line

Start by standing directly behind your ball, facing your target, looking over the ball towards the target. Establish an imaginary line from the middle of your ball to the middle of your target. This line is called the 'ball-to-target line'. As your target will normally be a reasonable distance away from you, and it will be difficult to keep a good fix on it as you move to take up your position at the ball, you will find it helps to pick out something on your ball-to-target line to aim your shot over. This is called your 'forward marker' – it could be a leaf, an old divot, a twig or a broken tee – anything you can see clearly. You will find it much easier to aim over your forward marker two to three yards away than towards a target 200 yards in the distance.

You should now find it reasonably easy to walk towards your ball and place the leading edge of your club at 90 degrees to your ball-to-target line. You have achieved the correct aim.

▲ The shoulders, waist, feet and club head should all be square to the target line.

MUST KNOW

Aiming the club

The correct aim of the club is when you establish a 90-degree relationship between the leading edge and the ball-to-target line, i.e. the imaginary line from the middle of the ball to the middle of the target.

◀ Using a forward marker, aim your club correctly at your intended target.

Grip

The grip refers to the position of your hands on the handle of the club, not the strength with which you grasp it. When you perfect your grip, you will feel as though the club is almost an extension of your arms and body which you can 'feel' throughout your golf swing.

A natural position

If you are holding the club correctly, it will become an extension of your hands and arms, and whatever your hands do will be reflected and extended by the club. The grip you choose will depend on several factors: your age, strength and the size of your hands. You need to develop a good grip as it controls the way in which your hands help generate club head speed in your swing and this, in turn, affects the distance you hit the ball. The swing path of the club head is also influenced by your grip, determining whether or not the club face will be square at impact and whether the ball will fly straight. Building a good grip will make hitting a ball much easier.

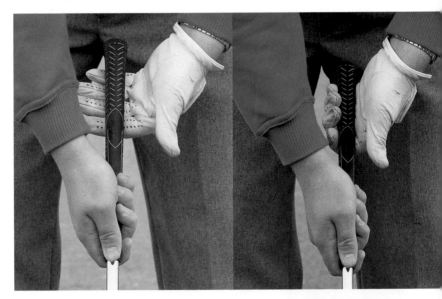

▲ Lay the club in the mid-knuckle point of the left hand. The ridge at the back of most grips will drop easily into it. Now wrap the fingers of the left hand around the grip of the club.

Types of grip

There are several grips that golfers use, ranging from the overlapping, or Vardon, grip to the interlocking and baseball grips. You should select the one that suits you best but it is important that both your hands work together in unison when you are taking a shot. The overlapping grip is the most popular and is suitable for golfers with large or average size hands whereas the interlocking grip is better suited to people with short fingers as it links the hands together. many beginners start off with the 'two-handed' baseball grip because it is the easiest and most natural way to grip a golf club, but if you want to lower your handicap and achieve maximum distance it is better to adopt another grip.

▲ The left-hand line, or 'V', should point up to the right shoulder from the left thumb and left side of the palm.

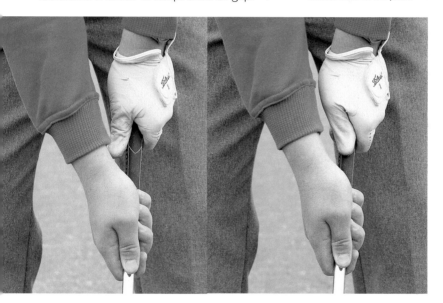

▲ Wrap the upper part of the left hand around the shaft of the club so that the left pad wraps over the grip and clasps it. Place the left thumb pointing down the top right-hand quarter of the grip with the 'V' in line with the right shoulder.

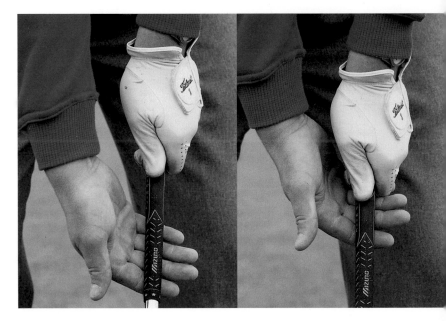

MUST KNOW

Grip key facts

● The aim of the grip is to establish the placing of your hands on the club by the method shown.

● You should also achieve a good degree of comfort in the correct holding position.

▲ Now place the club in the mid-knuckle point of the right hand and then move it up the grip towards the left hand as shown in the photographs above.

Practice drill

Go through the procedure shown of building your grip from start to finish, waggle the club around a little, take your hands off the club, and then repeat the whole process again. Repeat this five times, remembering the waggle at the end, and after the fifth time take a rest.

Practise this drill two or three times a day and in no time at all you will become accustomed to the position your hands should adopt on the club and will accomplish the right position and feel without even thinking about the process.

Which grip should you use?

The baseball grip is often the best for young junior golfers as it is suitable for small fingers and generates greater grip strength. Players with larger hands should try the overlapping or

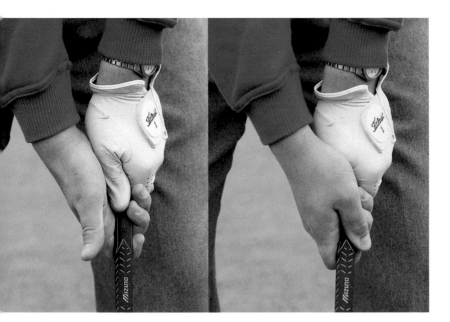

interlocking grip. Senior golfers often find that their grip strength and feel decreases with age and may need to modify their normal grip accordingly. Women may use any of the grips.

▲ Now overlap or interlock the little finger of the right hand with the index finger of the left hand. The lifeline of the left hand should cover the left thumb from top to bottom. The right thumb creates a 'V' or line with the right shoulder.

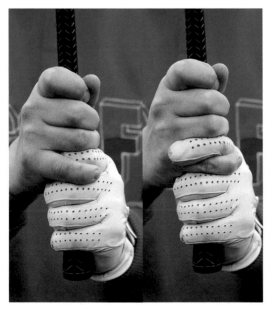

◄ These photographs show the overlapping Vardon grip (left) and the interlocking grip (right). In the Vardon grip, the little finger of the right hand overlaps the forefinger of the left hand. In the interlocking grip, the forefinger of the left hand interlocks with the little finger of the right hand. This grip is best for people with small hands.

Ball position

The ball must be positioned in the forward half of the stance (halfway between the centre of your feet and your front foot) for all normal shots. This makes the back of the ball available for you to strike, and places you in a position where you will be encouraged to use your body weight correctly through the swing.

▲ To establish the correct ball position, stand with feet together (left). Move your left foot into the correct position in relation to the ball (centre), then establish the stance width by moving your right foot (right).

◄ Feet should be parallel to the target line with the ball forward in your stance.

▲ The ball should be in the middle of your stance forwards in the hitting zone.

Body alignment

You must position your body in relation to your target. You should align your toes, knees, hips and shoulders parallel to the ball-to-target line. This ensures that your swing will direct the ball towards the target.

Practice drill

Place two clubs on the ground, one running parallel to your ball-to-target line and one at right angles to it. They should make a 'T' shape and there should be a gap of about 30 cm (12 in) between them. Face the shaft, which is running parallel with your ball-to-target line, making sure that your toes, knees, hips and shoulders are parallel to it. Use the other shaft running back between your feet to indicate the position of the ball, and make sure that this is halfway between the centre of your feet and your left foot. This is the ideal position for a medium iron.

▲ You will find any lines placed on the ground parallel to your target line a great help during practice.

▲ It is very important to position your shoulders parallel to the ball to target line, so it makes sense to keep your toes, knees and hips parallel too.

Posture

This is the positioning of your body at set up. Good posture is very important as it will establish a stable, balanced position from which you can move freely; the correct distance between you and the ball; and the correct angle of swing to produce a solid strike on the back of the ball. The golf swing is an athletic movement involving practically every part of your body. The posture position is the final link in your set up and must place you in readiness for that free athletic movement.

MUST KNOW

Why you need good posture
• To establish a position that will give you the opportunity to move freely and to remain balanced during your swing.
• To establish the correct distance between you and the ball.
• To establish the correct angle of swing.

▲ Good posture is the key to balanced movement and an effective golf swing. Keep your chin up (top) away from your torso and your back straight (above).

▲ The correct posture: bend forward from your hips until the club touches the ground, then flex your knees.

The swing

Having established the correct set up, you are ready to swing the golf club itself. The purpose of your swing is to generate power but many new, untrained golfers hurl themselves around so much in an attempt to do this that they have little chance of hitting the ball properly, far less sending it in the correct direction. This is quite natural.

Accuracy and control

When you stands on a teeing ground for the first time and look down the fairway, what is the first thing in your mind? Usually, how far away the flag seems. The next question is, 'How do I manage to hit the ball that far?' Most beginners think the answer is to hit it really hard.

So, without the proper training, it is very easy for you, as a new golfer, to fall into the bad habit of trying to hit the ball much too hard. This will make it difficult to control any of the actions that you are trying to make. Power has taken over and any accuracy and control could well be lost for ever. Do not let this happen to you.

You will achieve far more distance from a ball struck well with less power than from a ball that is struck badly but with more power. Take your time and never force a shot in an attempt just to hit it further. Always think of hitting the ball better, not harder!

▲ To achieve distance from a good shot, think about your target and where you want the ball to land.

MUST KNOW

Co-ordinate your movement

To swing the club well means that you will generate power whilst giving yourself a reasonable opportunity to strike the ball accurately and send it in the correct direction. This demands a well balanced, co-ordinated movement marrying together the two areas of power generation: your body action, and the areas you will be working on, firstly to understand them and then train yourself to put them into practice.

Body action

It is essential that you use your body correctly if you want to build a good swing. It is the biggest source of power in the swing, and how it moves will influence how well you are able to swing your arms, hands and club.

The pivoting motion

Your body action will determine how you use your large muscles; how much power you generate; how your arms, hands and club combine to create an effective swing; and the pace of your swing.

You need a good pivoting motion as well as the correct weight transfer during your swing. The pivoting action of your body helps return the club head consistently to the ball. Together with your weight transfer, it will generate the power needed to hit the ball the distance you require.

Your body will pivot and move your weight into your right side during the backswing. Then your body pivots into and around your left side, transferring your weight, through impact, on to your left foot by the end of your swing.

▲ A good pivoting action will help to generate power in your golf swing.

▼ Practise your pivoting motion without a club. You may find it helpful to do this in front of a mirror.

Backswing pivot

As your body starts to turn, your weight shifts on to your right foot, moving more into your right side. Keep the flex in your right knee constant so your weight stays directly above your right foot. Your shoulders should have turned over 90 degrees from the starting position. Your hips should have turned 30–40 degrees, and 75 per cent of your body weight should be over your right foot.

Don't keep your head too still; let it turn a little to the right. At the end of the backswing, your right thigh and the left side of your back should feel a little tense – indicative of the power stored up ready to use when striking the ball.

The downswing

Move the whole of your left side smoothly across until 50 per cent of your weight is on your left foot. Start turning your upper left side behind you, bringing more your weight on to your left foot as the pivot continues. Your right side will be pulled through by the movement of your left. At the end of the swing, your right shoulder will be closer to the target than your left, your hips will be at 90 degrees to the ball-to-target line, and 90 per cent of your weight will be over your left foot with only the toe of your right foot on the ground.

Your head should finish looking down the target line. Throughout the swing the angle of your spine, created at set up, should stay constant.

MUST KNOW

Body action key points
- Maintain your balance throughout the swing.
- Maintain the spinal angle throughout the swing.
- Control your weight transfer smoothly.
- Create controlled power.
- Control the speed of the swing.

▲ Practising the pivoting action helps you to develop the feel of the golf swing. You need to focus on achieving a 90-degree pivot back and through. Notice how this affects your weight transfer and balance. You should maintain the spine angle throughout.

The backswing

Now it is time to look at the swing in detail and to analyze the different parts so you can learn how to build a good, consistent swing. The first part of the movement, the backswing, is the preparation for the swing itself.

▲ If your body is in the correct position at the top of the backswing, you are more likely to produce an equally good downswing and follow through and hit a successful shot.

Pre-swing routine

To create an effective swing, you must position both yourself and the ball in the correct direction and in a powerful fashion. If you complete the backswing correctly, then the forward swing has a good chance of being equally successful. It is helpful to develop a pre-swing routine. Just before you start swinging the club, there are a couple of helpful movements that you can make: the waggle and the forward press.

● **Waggle** This is designed to help prevent you 'freezing' over the ball. It is a good idea to build this movement into your swing routine in order to help alleviate any tension in your body before swinging the club. A slight movement of the wrists taking the club back and forth on either side of the ball will help to ease the pressure. So before you make your swing, shift your weight slightly from foot to foot to relax your feet and legs.

● **Forward press** A smooth takeaway will lead to a more controlled swing. It does not have to be slow but it must be smooth or in tempo (below).

MUST KNOW

The speed of the golf swing

This is determined by how long it takes the large muscles to reach the top of the backswing, so if you are aware of arriving at the top you have performed the swing at a speed you can control. This allows you to find your own tempo. It does not matter if your tempo is quick, medium or slow – it is the swing that controls the rhythm.

To encourage this, a slight forward movement of the hands and wrists, while leaving the club head on the ground behind the ball, will create a recoil and thus trigger the backswing. It can also be achieved by a slight 'kicking in' of the right knee, again creating the recoil. If you find it difficult to get started in the backswing, you should spend some time experimenting with both systems and select the one that works best for you.

Achieving direction and power

A successful golf shot requires two elements: direction and power. You need to look in detail at the movements you have to make to encourage both of these things to happen so that you can build a routine that will eventually lead to a consistent swing. It is advisable to start off with a 6 or 7 iron. These clubs will make the ball travel far enough to let you see what you have achieved. They are not power clubs, which are designed to send the ball a long way, so there is no pressure on you to hit the ball really hard or smash the living daylights out of it.

Shoulder turn

If, at waist level, you discover that your shoulders have not turned enough, then you have taken the club head to the far side of the ball-to-target line. This often happens when the club has been picked up or lifted by the wrists or a bending of the elbows.

▼ Weight transfer is very important in your swing. It mimics a throwing action where your weight is transferred from one side of the body to the other as you swing through the strike: weight back, weight through.

MUST KNOW

At waist level

● The leading edge of the club head will be at right angles to the shoulders.

● The number of knuckles visible on the back of the left hand will be the same as in the set up.

● If your shoulders have turned in advance of the hands, the club head has been brought inside the line too quickly.

The takeaway

The club is taken straight back from the ball, close to the ground, for the first 12–15 cm (5–6 in). The club head will be on the target line parallel to the shoulders. You should feel the club head, shaft, left hand, arm and shoulder moving as one unit. Waist level is sometimes referred to as a 'half swing' where the shoulders have turned through approximately 45 degrees. If you were aligned correctly in the set up, and you are in this position, you should achieve good direction.

The second half

Complete the backswing by turning until the left shoulder is between the chin and the ball. The shoulders will have turned through approximately 90 degrees. The weight will be over the right hip, knee and ankle. You will feel torsion around the hips and inside of the left leg, and the hips will have rotated 45 degrees. Releasing this coiled tension produces the hit. You may lift your left heel off the ground if wished. The shoulders and legs have been fully used; this spring-like effect is ready to 'explode' into action on the downswing.

The downswing

Initiate this with your legs. Transferring the weight to the left leg will start the club moving downwards on the correct inside attack. The hands and arms will then take over to deliver the club head back to the ball.

Delivering the club head

This is done by uncocking the wrists while the arms continue to swing the club down. Your left arm maintains its firmness, giving your swing a good arc width and enabling you to build up effective club head speed to propel the ball a long way. As your right arm starts to straighten out, it generates yet more club head speed.

Meanwhile, from the top of the backswing, your raised left foot will lower itself immediately to the ground due to the lateral movement of your legs. Both feet will stay firmly on the turf throughout impact with the ball. They are the foundation of a smooth, solid swing. Keep your balance; if you lose it, you are trying too hard.

As you swing down, the speed of the downswing will get gradually faster until the wrists start to uncock, delivering the club head to the ball at tremendous speed.

Impact

At impact, the left side of your body will turn fractionally to the left but you will not achieve maximum club head speed until both your arms become straight just after contact with the ball to give maximum power through the hit.

MUST KNOW

Contact

● With medium and short irons, contact with the ball should occur just before the bottom of the swing.
● With long irons and fairway woods, contact should be at the bottom of the swing.
● With a driver, you should strike the ball slightly on the upswing.

Making good contact

Your posture at impact should mirror what it was at address. Don't try to lift the ball or scoop it up; the club's loft will do this for you. The way the club face strikes the ball is very important so focus on producing the right contact. You should aim to swing the club head through a circle from the top of the backswing, brushing the ground at the exact spot where the ball is sitting. A good-looking swing is no good unless contact is accurate.

Keep it together

Remember that your feet should stay in contact with the ground through impact, giving your swing a solid foundation. Your whole body is working together as one to hit the ball as hard as you can. You must not allow any one part of your body to become dominant.

The follow through

From impact, the club will continue to swing freely through the swing plane until it comes to a halt with the shaft behind your head at the top of the follow through. You should be in a well-balanced position.

After impact

Your body turns to the left together with the club face and the path of your swing. The left arm bends downwards slightly and your right shoulder comes through under your chin. This helps keep the swing on a wide arc through the hitting area and high into the follow through. Your body turns fully to the left and your chest and hips should face the target as you finish.

A balanced finish

To free the swing to carry on to an even higher finish, your head should rise naturally as your right shoulder hits your chin. Your right foot is pulled up on to the toes due to the right side pulling up through the follow through. It is very important to maintain tempo and achieve a balanced finish with good control of the club.

MUST KNOW

Swing guide
- There should not be any independent movement in your arms and hands.
- The plane of the swing is the key to striking the ball consistently and correctly.
- Your arms and hands should keep moving on the swing plane throughout.

Other clubs

Once you have mastered swinging a mid-iron, you need to learn how to use your other clubs. You will have to make slight adjustments to your weight distribution, width of stance and ball position when using different clubs. Other adjustments in your set up and swing will follow automatically from these.

Types of clubs

Golf clubs can be split into three groups:

- The mid-irons (5, 6 and 7).
- The woods and long irons.
- The short irons.

▼ When hitting a shot with your longer clubs, you need to produce a sweeping swing to make the ball fly further. Keep it smooth and unhurried – you don't have to hit the ball harder to make it travel a long way.

The woods and long irons consist of all the woods and the 1, 2, 3 and 4 irons. The short irons are the 8, 9, pitching wedge and sand iron. At this stage, don't even think of using a 1 or 2 wood or a 1 or 2 iron. These are the most difficult clubs.

Woods and long irons

Your longer clubs are designed to develop more momentum and thereby send the ball further even though you keep your swing the same as for the mid irons. The only adjustments you need make are to your set up and stance. Do not be tempted to force these shots. All you need to do is to make some minor modifications for the club you are using and then swing as you have already learned with your mid irons.

Adjust your stance

These clubs have longer shafts and create more momentum; hence they require a more stable stance than for your mid irons to maintain your stability and balance.

The length of shaft also affects the arc of your swing, making it slightly shallower. Therefore you need to create a more sweeping type of strike. To take all this into account, you will need to widen your stance fractionally and adjust the ball position. This will change your weight

MUST KNOW

Swing slowly

Many golfers swing too hard with their long clubs, trying to hit the ball over super-human distances. Because the shaft is longer and the club head travels on a bigger arc, you need to make a slower swing. A smooth unhurried one is always best.

▼ Follow through with your wood and feel your weight transferring from your right to your left side.

distribution at set up. Stand with your feet apart so that if you drew a line down from the inside of each arm it would then extend to the inside of each foot. You should position the ball opposite the inside of your left heel. This will have the effect of your weight distribution being 55 per cent on your right foot and 45 per cent on your left foot.

Practise your set up and swing

Now that you have made all the necessary changes to your stance, you should follow your normal set-up routine and practise swinging the club from this slightly different position. Always follow your full set-up drill and you will soon get used to the small changes required to use the longer clubs and will make them automatically without having to think about it.

Short irons

These clubs are specially designed to give the ball a high floating style of flight so that it will stop more quickly on the green. Because they have a shorter shaft, they will not send the ball as far as your mid-irons. Use them to play shorter, more lofted shots, such as out of the rough.

Stance and set up

Narrow the width of your stance so an imaginary line extending down from the inside of each arm ends on the outside of each foot. This provides the correct stability and mobility for short shots. You should feel slightly more weight on your left foot. Aim for a weight distribution of 55 per cent on your left foot and 45 per cent on your right. This will give you the correct angle of swing.

Now set up in the usual way; adjusting your width of stance and weight distribution are all that are needed. Check your posture and swing in the normal way for an iron shot.

MUST KNOW

Less mobility
The narrower stance means that your body is less mobile for the short iron shots.

Fairway woods

The fairway woods, which include the 3, 4, 5, 7 and 9 woods, are more lofted and easier to use than the straighter-faced long irons, making them increasingly popular with golfers of all abilities and handicaps.

The set up

The wide sole of the club should sit flat on the ground with the ball positioned opposite your left heel and your hands level or just slightly behind the back of the ball. This adjustment to your usual set up, when combined with the long shaft of the club, helps you to produce a sweeping arc of contact on the ball rather than the more downward contact you create with an iron.

To check your set up, ground your fairway wood on a hard, flat surface with the club face aiming down the target line. Check the angle of the shaft. Hold the club lightly in the fingers of one hand; do not grip it. Now start building your stance around the club and take your grip.

Wind conditions

These should be considered before selecting a fairway wood as opposed to a long iron. A 5 wood, for example, will tend to flight the ball on a higher trajectory than a 2 or 3 iron. When playing into a strong wind, play a long iron to prevent the ball travelling too high into the air.

▲ The sole of the wood is sitting flat in the correct position. Note the angle of the shaft (top). The incorrect way to ground a wood (above). The back edge is up and the loft on the face has been reduced to zero.

▲ It is better to use fairway woods when playing from the semi-rough as they can sweep more easily and cleanly through the grass than a long iron club.

Playing in semi-rough

Your fairway woods are useful where the grass is longer in the semi-rough. They will tend to sweep cleanly through the grass whereas it may grab and twist a long iron club. However, you should always be cautious if the ball is sitting down really low in the grass. Sometimes it is better to stay safe and be less ambitious. Rather than try and hit any long club, the safe percentage shot would be a lofted short iron club.

The golden rule is that it is safe to use a fairway wood if the club can contact the ball below its equator. This makes it suitable for hitting from most reasonably good grassy lies just off the fairway. In order to strike the ball cleanly away, contact must occur at the bottom of the swing.

Using woods

You must be able to strike the ball below its equator if you are to use a wood. To use a 3 wood from the fairway you will need a good lie with the whole of the ball sitting above the turf.

▲ If the ball is nestling low down in the grass, you can hit it with a fairway wood or choose to play safe and use a more lofted short iron.

The long game

You will gain great satisfaction from developing a sound long game and hitting accurate shots with a wood or long iron, but first you need to learn how to produce a consistently reliable swing in order to master the longer-shafted, straighter-faced clubs, which are more difficult to control than mid irons.

Using different clubs

You don't have to learn a different swing for each club, but the distance you stand from the ball and where you position it in your stance will need to be adjusted according to the length and design of the club you are using. Because hitting shots with the long irons and woods is more difficult, you must practise to achieve consistency and accuracy. So start off with the middle clubs and then progress to longer ones as you improve.

SELECTING THE RIGHT CLUB

There are a number of specific factors that you need to consider before you finally select the right club for each golf shot. Read through the following guidelines to choosing the right club:
- Wind direction and strength (especially on exposed courses).
- Temperature: a warm ball travels up to 20 yards further than a cold ball.
- Ground firmness: will the ball stop quickly or run, and if so how much?
- A backdrop of trees or a bank behind the green will have a tendency to make it look closer than it really is.
- If there is no background behind the green, there will be a tendency to give the impression that it is further than it is.
- The size of the green: large greens will look closer whereas small greens will look further away than they actually are.
- The length of the flagsticks have a similar visual effect: long ones will look closer whereas short ones will look further away.
- There may be 'dead ground', especially if you are playing over mounds.
- Work on knowing the distance that you can hit each club.

Club/yardage chart

Yards	110	120	130	140	150	160	170	180	190	210	225	240
Irons	PW	9	8	7	6	5	4	3	2			
Woods								5	4	3	2	1

Judging distance

In order to select the correct club to hit the ball to the target, you need to be able to judge the distance it needs to travel. Your should know, within 10 yards, how far you can hit each club. Of course, when you are starting out, you must expect some mishits that do not fly far enough, but you should choose a club on the basis that you will hit a good shot.

Practice drill

Gather together about 20 balls of the same make, the type you would normally use for playing. On the practice ground, hit all the balls with a mid iron (say, a 6 or 7 iron) and then pace out the distance to the spot where a group of good shots have landed. If you make your strides a yard each in length, you can calculate how far you hit with that iron.

Now repeat the exercise with each of your other irons. There should be approximately 10 yards between each club. If your 6 iron goes 150 yards, a 7 iron should go 140 yards, and a 5 iron 160 yards. You need your irons for the accurate approach shots, whereas your woods are the distance clubs. They will have a greater differential with about 20 yards between clubs.

▲ Instead of rushing your shot, take your time to look at your target and work out the distance the ball must fly in order to reach it.

Yardage charts

Most courses issue a pre-measured course planner showing the distance to the centre or front of each green, although it is always wise to check this measurement out for yourself.

Split the distance down

Before playing a shot, stand slightly to the side in order to estimate the distance between you and your target. This is easier than judging it from behind the ball. Now split the distance down into two or three sections so that you can visualize a 50-yard mark, followed by another 50-yard mark. By adding these together, it is possible to build up a more accurate picture rather than just looking from behind the ball straight at the target.

▲ You may find it useful to stand to the side of your intended line and, in your mind, divide the distance the ball must fly into two or three equidistant parts.

Your target clubs

The medium irons – the 5, 6 and 7 irons – are the target clubs which are normally used for approaching the green from about 130–170 yards away. You should never hit a ball flat out with a medium iron. Before making your final choice of club, try to assess the flag position and whether more trouble lies in front of or behind the green.

Set up for medium irons

For your set up, position the ball 7–10 cm (3–4 in) inside the left heel with your hands slightly forward of the ball so that the club shaft and your left arm are in line (looking from the front, not the side). For the grip for medium irons, you should position your hands normally with 4 cm (1¹/₂ in) showing at the top of the grip.

Playing in the wind

Always use the wind to your advantage rather than fight it. If you are playing into a left-to-right wind, don't try and draw the shot. Instead, set up to allow for the wind and then play a normal straight shot which the wind will move back to

▲ In the set up the ball is inside the left heel and the left arm and club shaft are in line (top). Position your hands normally on the grip (above) with 4 cm (1¹/₂ in) showing at the top.

▲ When playing into the wind, choke down the grip, leaving 7–10 cm (3–4 in) showing at the top. Use this grip when you play low punch shots, half shots and recoveries from trees.

the target. You need to visualize your target – in this case, left of its actual position – and then you should swing towards your imagined target.

When playing into or across the wind, use a larger club than normal, swing a little shorter and do not force it. A wider stance will help you to maintain balance and tends to restrict the amount of body turn and therefore the length of the swing. Use the same principles as when playing a low shot.

MUST KNOW

Wind direction
To judge the wind direction, you should:
● Look at the flag.
● Take a look at the tree tops.
● Lastly, hold up a handkerchief.

◀ When playing a shot from a bad lie where there is too much grass between the club face and the ball, use a middle to short club rather than a long iron or a wood.

want to know more?
Take it to the next level...

Go to...
▶ **Playing a round** – page 132
▶ **Curing swing faults** – page 152
▶ **Golf rules and etiquette** – page 172

Other sources
▶ **Your local golf professional**
   for professional swing instruction
▶ **Your local driving range**
   for practising hitting balls
▶ **Internet**
   golf swing software programmes
▶ **Golf Tour Pro videos**
   for swing masterclasses
▶ **Publications**
   visit www.collins.co.uk for Collins golf books

Bad lies
If you hit an off-line tee shot which lands in a bad lie, the medium irons are good for playing back on to the fairway. The best club to use when the ball is down in thick rough and you can only see the top is a 7 iron. This is because the shorter shaft gives a steeper swing, and there is sufficient loft to get the ball airborne with forward movement.

overcoming

hazards

There are many situations on a course that are hazardous, but the only things that are classified as hazards are sand and water. Trees, the rough, uneven lies, grass hollows and banks are featured here because you will encounter these obstacles and will need to modify your normal swing in order to pull off a special shot that will help you recover from an awkward position.

In the rough

If your ball ends up in the rough, you must decide whether the lie is so severe that it prevents you playing a club long enough to reach the green. If this is the case, do not take risks; play a safety shot out to the middle of the fairway.

Take a risk or play safe?

Beginners often hit their ball into trouble and are then tempted to go for a miracle recovery shot. Although they may succeed gloriously 10 per cent of the time, the other 90 per cent they will end up in worse trouble. You must learn when to take a calculated risk and when to play safe.

Texture

The texture of the rough will affect the club head in numerous ways as you swing through it. Be aware that there will be more resistance and a tendency to twist as the club head contacts the rough and the ball. Allow for this by making your grip firmer than usual, especially in the top three fingers of your left hand. The rough will grab the hosel of the club, causing the club face to close

▲ The ball is sitting down, or plugged; direct club to ball contact is impossible. So take a lofted club and hit down into the ground and the ball.

DIFFERENT SORTS OF LIES IN THE ROUGH

You need to recognize the following different lies in order to use the correct golf technique when you are tackling each one.
● **Good lie:** This is easy to spot but you must take care to observe which way the grass is growing. If it lies in the same direction as you are going to swing, it is a good lie. It may be better to use a wood than a long iron as it will slide easily through long grass.
● **Normal lie:** You can see the ball but it is low down in longish grass, which will get between your club face and the ball at impact. A wood may be better but if you use an iron, increase your grip pressure for better club control.
● **Bad lie:** The ball nestles down very low in long grass, almost obliterated from view. Use a very lofted club, such as a wedge, to drive the club head down and through the ball, lifting it back on to the fairway.

at impact and the ball to fly left of your target. To allow for this, you should aim 10–15 yards right of your target with both the club face and your feet.

Lower ball flight

The club face will not make direct contact with the ball and some grass will be trapped between the two, creating a cushioning effect and making the ball respond differently. It will tend to fly lower and shoot forwards with loss of control and without any backspin on landing. You can allow for this by taking a more lofted club than usual and playing the ball further towards your right foot. This will have the effect of producing a steeper downward angle of attack on the ball which has more chance of success. There is a risk that the club head will turn over at impact and smother the shot as the hosel and shaft become entangled in the grass, but your firmer grip and open club face at address should help to prevent this happening.

Ball sitting up high

Occasionally, the ball will sit up high on top of the rough and then you can use a straighter-faced club, such as a 4 iron. Position the ball to the left in your stance and do not to ground your club too hard at address (and risk moving the ball). Take care that you do not hit underneath the ball taking the grass below it. Instead, hold the club head in such a way that you address the middle of the ball and produce a sweeping action; avoid a steep downward strike.

Ball in heather

This shot is always misleading as heather looks short but is very tough and wiry to play from. Do not be tempted to risk any kind of long shot, but take your penalty and then play a lofted 9 iron or wedge to move the ball back on to the fairway.

▲ When the ball is sitting up, do not press the club head down into the ground.

▲ When playing from wiry heather, use a lofted club and a firm grip. Play the shot in the same way as you would from deep rough.

Bunker shots

Bunkers can inspire instant fear in most beginners and high-handicappers, but usually their worries are needless because when they have mastered the basic technique for these shots, hitting the ball out of a bunker need not be difficult.

Bunker technique

This shot requires a different technique to any standard grass lie. It is the only shot where you should hit behind the ball and produce a slicing action whereby your swing path goes left of your target, and you hold the club face open (aimed to the right of your swing line) through impact. To execute good escape shots, you will need a sand wedge with not too large a flange and a rounded leading edge slightly ahead of the hosel.

▼ Your aim is to splash out a handful of sand and, with it, the ball. You should not try to strike the ball itself.

Addressing the ball

Your set up, stance and ball position for bunker shots need adjustment. Shuffle your feet into the sand to give your swing a firm base and test the depth and texture of the surface. Do not ground your club in the sand.

Your set up

Position your feet and body on a line 15-20 degrees left of your target with the ball opposite a spot just inside your left heel to encourage a steeper swing path travelling parallel to your body's aim, matching your open club face. Focus on a spot behind the ball and strike the sand 5 cm (2 in) before the ball so it floats out on a cushion of sand. Follow through with the weight on your left foot.

▲ When addressing the ball in a bunker, open your stance and ensure the club face is open. You should feel relaxed with the club shaft straight up towards you.

▲ The set up for bunker shots with the feet shuffled into the sand, just enough to cover the soles of your shoes.

▲ This set up shows two main faults: the club face is de-lofted and the ball is too far back in the stance.

MUST KNOW

Never ground your club

The Rules of golf prohibit you from grounding your club in a hazard. Avoid this by taking your grip on the club before entering a bunker and placing your thumbs down a line slightly to the left of the front of the grip to open the club face.

The stroke

Hitting good shots out of bunkers will save you strokes so it is well worth practising and perfecting them. The aim is to create quite a steep 'U'-shaped swing so the club head travels through the sand and out the other side in a long and relaxed follow through. Do not chop at the sand or the ball.

Your swing

Unlike other shots, your hands should not rotate through impact; keep your club face open. You should not feel direct contact with the ball. The cushion of sand between the club face and ball helps you take a long swing so the ball comes out slowly. Keep your swing speed steady; don't rush it. Regular practice will instill confidence. You must be relaxed to hit consistently well; that comes when you can execute the shot successfully.

Greenside bunkers

Greenside bunkers can be defined as those within reach of the pin in one shot. The height of the bunker lip is important; if necessary, come out of a bunker to the side or even backwards, wherever

▲ Your club should strike the sand behind the ball, about the length of a credit card, and travel through to a smooth follow through.

the lips are not so steep. Your feet and body should aim left of the target. Make a long swing, taking sand behind the ball and keeping the club face open at the bottom with no hint of stopping at the ball. The arms and club should move to the left of the target with the body facing to the left and a long follow through.

MUST KNOW

Bunker knowhow
When taking bunker shots, remember the following points:
- Open club face.
- Open stance.
- Aim and look at a spot a credit card's length behind the ball.
- Take some sand and follow through to shoulder height.

▲ A greenside bunker shot requires an open club face with the ball positioned forward in the stance.

▼ Set up with the feet and body aiming left of target. Make a long swing, taking sand before the ball and keeping the club face open at the bottom of the arc.

Downhill bunker shots

Set up with an open club face with the ball well back in your stance. Aim to hit a couple of inches behind the ball with your weight more on the left foot. The loft of your club will be reduced because of the slope and the club head should follow the contour of the sand with a steeper backswing and lower follow through. Your swing should be shorter for this shot so that the ball will come out lower with run.

▶ How to play a downhill bunker shot. Adopt a wider stance with more hip bend. Set up with the weight favouring the left leg so that your body is at right angles to the slope with the shoulders following the lie of the slope, and an open club face. Make an early wrist break to clear the back lip of the bunker and keep the forward swing low after contact. Your weight must stay on the left leg throughout with no hint of falling back. The ball trajectory will tend to be low.

Uphill bunker shots

These shots are tricky and therefore you must adjust your set up accordingly. Your weight should be more on the right side with your club face less open than for a normal shot. Aim to hit the sand only 1–2 cm (1/2–1 in) behind the ball and focus your eyes on this spot. Your club head should follow the contour of the sand, and the follow through will swing up more quickly. You will need to take a long forward swing because the ball will pop up higher rather than forwards. And don't forget afterwards to rake up the marks you have left in the bunker.

◄ To play an uphill bunker shot successfully, you should use an open stance with more weight on the right leg. Aim to take less sand before the ball and let the long forward swing follow the contour of the bunker. The ball will come out naturally with a high trajectory.

Long bunker shots

To hit the ball a long way from a fairway bunker, you need a flat lie without any ridges of sand just behind the ball. When you play this shot, you need a wide,sweeping swing and you must ensure that you take the ball first.

Set up and shot

When setting up for this shot, shorten down on the grip and address the ball halfway up. Make sure you select a club with sufficient loft to clear the bunker face. The feet should not be shuffled into the sand, and the sole of the club should be held level with the equator of the ball. Your arms and the club should move in unison to create a

▲ When you set up for a long bunker shot, you must shorten down on the grip.

▼ The correct backswing for a long bunker shot. Your feet should not be shuffled into the sand and your club should be an extension of your arms as they move together to create a wide, sweeping swing through the ball, not the sand.

OVERCOMING HAZARDS

wide, sweeping arc. Never try to force this shot; if
you attempt to hit the ball too hard it will result in
an inaccurate shot and higher scores.

Playing out of fairway bunkers

When playing out of a fairway bunker, try to put
all calculations of the distance to the green out
of your mind and just concentrate on making the
shot in hand correctly. Decide which club you
need to use to clear the lip of the bunker and
then focus on getting the ball into play in a single
shot. If you have a poor lie, play the shot as in a
greenside bunker, but if you have a good lie with
the ball sitting up cleanly, set up with a normal
ball position and make a controlled three-quarter
swing. You should not make contact with the
sand before the ball.

▲ The incorrect way to play
the long bunker shot with
the ball too far back in the
stance, the feet shuffled
into the sand and too early
a wrist break.

Plugged bunker shots

In this situation, the bottom of the ball is below the level of most of the sand in the bunker and you need a digging action, effected by the leading edge of the club, to explode the ball out and play the shot successfully.

The set up

The successful execution of this shot depends on experience and you will have to learn when to play it and when it is better to take a penalty drop. It is a good idea to spend some time practising this shot, with the ball in different positions, to enable you to find out what you can and cannot achieve. You may be amazed at the results.

▼ The stance for this stroke differs from a normal bunker shot. It is less open with the ball placed back towards the right foot. Do not lean backwards and try to scoop the ball out of a plugged lie. Concentrate on hitting down firmly in to the sand, allowing the club to explode the ball out.

▲ The ball position is slightly further back in the stance, causing a steeper backswing.

The swing

For this shot, especially if the ball is well buried, you must close the club face slightly – the end of the toe should be pointing at the ball. Your stance should be less open with the ball placed back towards the right foot. Make a steep takeaway with wrist break to create a steeper descending arc as you jab downwards into the sand and ball, with only 2 cm (1 in) sand before the ball. The ball will fly much lower than usual from this type of lie and will run on landing so you cannot control this shot effectively but you will have escaped!

Wet or dry sand

If the bunker is full of wet, firm sand rather than the soft, dry variety, you may need a sharp-edged 9-iron to cut through the sand and get you out of trouble. For normal dry sand, use a sand wedge.

Ball under the lip of a bunker

If you are confronted with an awkward lie where the ball is close to the overhanging lip of a bunker, you use the same basic technique as for the other bunker shots. You will need extra height and a steep downswing arc if you are to hit the ball cleanly out of the sand back on to the grass.

The set up

When you set up for this type of bunker shot you need a slightly more open stance than usual and you must position the ball further forward. This will give you extra height and effectively increase the loft of your club face. As always, keep your eyes focused on a spot in the sand behind the ball – in this case, 5–7 cm (2–3 in) behind it. If you focus on the ball itself, you will hit it too cleanly and thin it into the lip of the bunker. Make sure you concentrate on the right spot in the sand.

▼ Make a quick backswing with an early wrist break, then swing down at a sharp downward angle into the sand behind the ball. Do not try to scoop up the ball. The face of the bunker may prevent your full follow through.

▲ Set up with an open stance, the club face well open and the ball position forward in your stance.

The swing

With your weight on the right side, you should swing the club head up quickly with an early wrist break to the full backswing position. Your left arm will lead the downswing in a sharp downward attack into the sand about 5–7 cm (2–3 in) behind the ball. Throughout the forward swing, you should keep the club face open. Your hands and the club should move together in unison. As you swing down and through, your weight will transfer on to the left foot. Do not worry about lifting the ball and attempting to scoop it up out of the sand. Let your lofted club do the work for you.

You may find that you cannot make a full follow through and it will be restricted by the face of the bunker. However, don't worry if this happens. The ball will rise quickly out of the bunker on impact and by the time you reach this position it will be long gone so it will not matter if your club hits the bank.

Water and trees

Getting out of trouble is an intrinsic part of golf so do not panic if you are confronted with a tree-lined course or water hazard. Instead of seeing all the places where you do not want to hit the ball, focus on your target and try to visualize a positive shot with the ball landing in the right place.

Shade out the hazards

In your mind, shade out any hazard areas and just picture a perfect shot with the sun shining on your target. Light it up and see yourself hitting it. Banish negative thoughts and blot out the water in front of the green, the bunker trap lying in wait beside it and the clump of trees that stand obstinately in your way to the pin. You will find positions on every golf course that are not ideal and which require recovery shots.

▼ Visualize the sun shining on the fairway or green, depending on your target area. See yourself hitting it. If you fear your shot may land up in the ravine on the right or the trees it probably will.

▶ Think positively when you are playing over water. You should focus only on the job in hand: making good contact with the ball. Try to push any negative thoughts and fears right out of your mind.

Hitting from under trees

Although they may look beautiful on the golf course, trees are potential hazards, especially if your ball ends up under one. If so, you have two options: a low shot from underneath or a shot through a gap in the branches. Judging the ball flight through a gap is obviously very difficult so it is usually more sensible to go for a low shot.

Playing a low shot

Choose a relatively straight-faced club for this shot. The ball should be back in your stance opposite the mid point between your feet. Try not to hit the ball too hard; if you hit it softly, it will not have the opportunity to rise. You want to keep the ball flight low underneath the branches of the tree. So maintain your swing rhythm and keep your downswing very slow to make good contact with the ball.

MUST KNOW

Tree options
If there are some trees between you and the hole, you will have three options:
● Hit over the trees.
● Play around the right side of them with draw (see page 84).
● Play around the left side of them with fade (see page 82). These shots are quite advanced and, for most beginners, it is best just to play sideways, even if it means adding a shot, and then get back into play when you can see the target again.

◀ Two views of the address position for playing a low shot. To keep the ball flight low, position the ball further back in the stance as shown.

Shaping your shots: the fade

By learning how to shape your shots, you can play them around trees and hazards. The fade is an advanced shot but, with practice, you can master it and it will help get you out of some tricky situations around the course.

▲ When setting up for the fade, you should aim to the left with the ball just inside the left heel. Adjust your grip to maintain an open club face through impact.

Line of ball flight

Use the fade to move the ball from left to right but, before attempting it, stand behind the ball and visualize your shot, choosing the line on which you want the ball to start. Build your stance and alignment around this line because the swing path direction is the most powerful force and dictates where the ball flies initially.

Club selection and set up

To impart clockwise spin on the ball and make it bend to the right, you will need to select a fairly straight-faced club such as a 4 or 5 iron. Set up, aiming to the left with the ball just inside your left heel. For the grip, place both thumbs down on the grip just left of the centre line. When you look down you should see less of the back of your left hand, and more of the back of your right hand than normal.

▼ This swing sequence shows the correct technique for executing the fade. The balls on the ground indicate the flight path of the ball.

Fade or draw?

How do you decide when to play a left to right shot (a fade) or a right to left shot (a draw)? The following advice may help you to avoid playing the wrong shot at the wrong time.

- If you have a tight lie, play a fade.
- If the lie is good, you can play a draw.
- Never try to fade the short irons.
- It is easier to fade with a straighter club.

The swing

For the fade, your swing will be influenced by the lie of the ball. You will need a steep swing with an open club face at impact for hitting the ball from a tight lie. Your backswing should be straighter back than usual and the arms should swing across your body to finish left of your left shoulder on the follow through.

The set-up grip change will allow the club face to return in an open position, but keep the left hand leading. Be careful, you must not be tempted to rush this shot – approach it in a calm, considered way and make sure you take a smooth, slow swing.

▲ Keep the open position of the club face at impact to produce clockwise spin on the ball so that it moves from left to right in the desired way.

Shaping your shots: the draw

Before taking this shot where the ball flies from right to left, visualize the ball flight you need to avoid any trees or obstacles between you and your target. When you have chosen this path, it will become your target and you can adjust your stance and body alignment accordingly.

Club selection and set up

To create anti-clockwise (right to left) spin on the ball, contact it with a closed club face. This will reduce the loft so you should select a more lofted club than for a fade. Try using your 6 or 7 iron for this shot. Use a strong grip, both hands clockwise on the club (thumbs right of the centre line). As you look down, you will see more of the back of your left hand and less of the back of your right than normal.The club face should be closed with the ball positioned towards the back of the stance. Your feet and body should aim to the right. The ball will land with overspin causing more run, so allow for this.

OVERCOMING HAZARDS

84

▶ The balls on the ground show the right-to-left flight path of the ball.

Perfecting the draw

- Your feet and body should aim to the right.
- The club face should be toed in slightly (closed).
- Your hands should be further right on the grip.
- The ball should be towards middle of the stance.
- The backswing should be more rounded.
- Rotate forearms and hands through impact.
- Follow through towards the initial aim point.

The swing

For this shot, you should make your backswing more rounded so it travels on an inside curve. Your forearms and hands should rotate through impact and you should follow through towards your initial target point. Do not rush your swing but keep it smooth, rhythmic and unhurried on an in-to-out path. To get a draw, the club face should be slightly closed at impact.

▲ Through impact, the club face should be slightly closed and your forearms and hands should rotate.

Playing high shots

A high shot is useful when you need to clear obstacles such as trees, so use a sufficiently lofted club. Your aim is to get the ball back in play so don't take risks; you may well end up in an even worse position.

▲ Set up with the ball further forward in your stance.

▼ On the backswing use more wrist action. At impact you will feel the right hand working under the left. Make sure you keep your head still and behind the ball until after impact.

The set up and swing

You need a good lie for this shot. Set up with the ball further forward than normal in your stance, more towards your left foot. Your hands should be level or just behind the ball with the weight more on the right side. Your right shoulder should be lower than the left shoulder with your head behind the ball. Swing your arms higher in the backswing and when you swing through impact your weight should be more on the right side than normal.

MUST KNOW

Key points for a high shot

- The ball should be further forward in your stance.
- Your hands should be level with the ball.
- Your weight should favour the right leg.
- Keep your head still until after impact.
- Take a divot, and get to the bottom of the ball.

Playing low shots

Sometimes you may want to produce a low ball flight and a 5 or 6 iron is perfect for this, provided that you reduce the loft by keeping your hands forward of the club head through impact.

The set up and swing

When setting up for a low shot, the ball should be positioned towards the back of the stance with the hands well forward and your weight favouring the left side. The toe of the club face should be turned in. Choke down on the grip a little and make a wide swing to punch the ball forwards. The ball will travel a long way so a half to three-quarters swing is adequate. You should follow through with your hands, arms and club pointing at the target.

▲ Set up with the ball well back in your stance and the club face toed in slightly.

MUST KNOW

Key points for a low shot

- The ball should be towards your right foot.
- Your hands should be forward of the ball, and level with the middle of your left thigh.
- The club face should be toed in slightly.
- Your weight should favour the left leg.

▼ Choke down on the grip a little and make a wide, firm-wristed swing to punch the ball forwards and finish pointing towards the target.

Uneven lies

Out on the fairway, you will encounter a number of different lies: sloping, uphill and downhill. In order to make successful shots from slopes and trouble spots, you will need to make several changes to your set up and have a sound technique.

Ball above your feet

This shot has a tendency to fly right to left in a draw or hook shape. To execute this shot successfully, your posture in the set up should be straighter, with less bend from the waist. Do not push back on your heels too much. Move your hands lower down the club grip, making the playing length of your club shorter (choking down on the club), and always aim a little right of your target. The ball should always be positioned towards the centre of your stance.

▲ Position the ball in the centre of your stance and to the right as shown by the clubs on the ground.

▼ When you make your swing with the ball above the feet your posture should be straighter and the swing plane flatter. The more rounded swing should produce a shot that flies in the desired direction from right to left.

Choking down on the club

Due to a combination of swing path and face angle, this shot will have a tendency to fly from right to left and although it will go a similar distance to normal, the slope will bring it slightly closer to you at address. You can allow for this by moving your hands a little down the grip of the club, thereby making the playing length of the club shorter. This is commonly known as 'choking down on the club'.

The swing

To make contact with a ball that is above your feet, you must make a flatter, more rounded swing than usual on the backswing and follow through. This will have the effect of producing a right-to-left shot in a draw or hook shape. The ball will travel approximately the same distance as usual even though the slope has brought it nearer to you. If the lie is not too severe and you need distance, you could play a fairway wood.

▲ At address (above), do not bend your hips and knees too much (top). This will cause your hands to be too low and you will end up hitting a bad shot.

Ball below your feet

Many golfers detest playing this shot but if you make the right adjustments to your set up and keep your balance it is not difficult. Always take a practice swing in this situation before hitting your shot. It will help to give you a feel for the shot as well as being a way of testing your balance.

The set up

This is an awkward stance with the ball lower than normal, so you should stand a little closer than usual, positioning the ball forward in your stance towards your left foot. Bend more from your hips than your knees but increase your knee flex to maintain your balance and enable you to get down to the ball. Aim to the left of your target and use a longer club than normal, holding it at full length and gripping it at the end. Your hands should be a little in front of the ball at address. More of your weight will be towards your toes so

▲ At address bend more from your hips and aim to the left. Flex your knees to maintain your balance.

▼ For this shot, you should bend more from your hips and aim to the left. Your backswing should be more upright with a low spine angle through impact with the ball to create a balanced follow through.

Keep your balance

For this shot, you must bend forwards from your hips, using your knees to maintain your balance. You may find this difficult as it is easy to lose your balance and fall forwards towards the ball. Practise this often, swinging smoothly, and you will soon master the delicate balancing position and hit good shots.

you must retain enough over your heels to keep your balance. Try not to feel as though you are going to topple forwards towards the ball.

The swing

Your swing plane will be more upright and you must retain the spine angle to stay low through impact. The correct posture will make a more balanced follow through possible. The ball flight will tend to go from left to right, which will cause the ball to fade and lose distance so you should use a less lofted club than normal. Do not try to hit the ball too hard; you should feel as though you are punching it away with your hands and arms.

▲ Keep your balance for this shot and be careful to avoid overswinging.

Uphill lies

This is a lie where the ball is positioned on an upslope, sloping towards the target. It is a relatively easy shot to play because the uphill slope doubles as your very own launching pad to get the ball airborne.

▲ The correct set up when playing from an uphill lie. Note how the body weight corresponds with the slope, favouring the right leg.

The set up and swing

Your body weight should be parallel with the slope, favouring the right leg (lower foot). Use a less lofted club and aim slightly right of your intended target. Position the ball forwards in your stance towards your left foot (the higher one).

Your swing angle into the ball must correspond with the slope, so your follow through must rise more quickly so as not to bury the club into the ground. The slope and your body weight staying back on your right side will cause the ball to fly

▼ When you swing, allow for the change in ball flight by aiming slightly right of your intended target. Move the ball forwards in your stance and shift more of your body weight to your lower foot before taking your normal swing.

Very steep uphill and downhill lies

In these situations where the slope is very severe, your balance can be in real jeopardy. Your best bet is to play the ball back to a flat piece of ground and start again. Use only a small swing with a more lofted club, but keep your aim and ball position the same as for playing from normal uphill and downhill lies.

much higher, and you will tend to pull it to the left, hence your aim adjustment.

It is important throughout this shot to focus on maintaining good balance and rhythm and to play within your capabilities – do not attempt to emulate your golfing heroes on the Tour and try to pull off a miracle shot. Just adapt your usual technique slightly, as described above, in order to accommodate the slope.

▲ An incorrect set up when playing from an upslope. The weight is leaning into the slope and the ball is too far back in the stance.

Downhill lies

This is exactly the opposite of an uphill lie; it is a lie where the ball is on a downslope, sloping down towards the target. Because the slope is pointing downwards, it is more difficult to get the ball airborne.

Set up and club selection

When playing this shot, you must not try and lift the ball, so choose a 5 iron or a more lofted club which will become less lofted as a result of the way in which the slope influences how you stand. When you are setting up for this shot, it is important that you allow for the flight of the ball, and accommodate the slope.

Your body weight should be parallel with the slope with your spine set at right angles to it, favouring the left leg – do not lean back into the slope. Your right shoulder should feel higher than the left. Aim slightly to the left of your target as the ball will curve to the right in flight. Position the ball towards the centre of your stance, more towards your higher foot.

▲ An incorrect set up from a downslope, leaning back into the slope with the ball too far forwards.

▼ Set up with your body weight corresponding with the slope and favouring the left leg. Maintaining your rhythm and balance is the key to success with this tricky shot. Make sure you use a lofted club to get the ball airborne.

MUST KNOW

Club selection
Do not attempt to
hit the ball with a
straight-faced club off
a downslope. A 5 iron
is about the longest
club that you should
contemplate using,
unless you are very
proficient at this shot.

◄ On your backswing, the
club head should go back
more quickly. As it descends
to the ball and through impact
it should follow the slope.

The swing

Your club head should start to rise more quickly
on the backswing and follow the line of the slope
on returning to the ball. Stay lower after the ball
to correspond with the slope. The inevitable
result is a lower flying shot and there will be a
tendency for the ball to fade from left to right.

want to know more?

Take it to the next level...

Go to...
▶ **Pitching out of bunkers** – page 128
▶ **Playing a round** – page 132
▶ **Golf rules and etiquette** – page 183

Other sources
▶ **Your local golf professional**
   for lessons on overcoming hazards
▶ **Videos and DVDs**
   for specialist teaching on hazards
▶ **Internet**
   interactive CD-ROMs
▶ **Golf seminars**
   specialist instruction on hazards
▶ **Publications**
   visit www.collins.co.uk for Collins golf books

perfect

putting

The average round of golf is composed of 37 per cent long game and 63 per cent short game, so good putting can lower your scores. The skills needed are touch and feel, making it possible for the slightest woman to compete on equal terms with even the strongest man. Practising your putting regularly will help improve your game rapidly.

The putting grip

Good preparation is the key to successful golf, and putting is no exception to this rule. You need to perfect an effective and consistent relationship between your hands and the way you place them upon the handle of your putter. Your putting grip will be slightly different from the one you normally use for full shots, and you must decide which one to use.

The overlapping grip

There are several ways of holding a putter. Some golfers favour the overlapping, or Vardon, grip where all the fingers of the left hand are placed around the handle, with the thumb lying on top of the handle and the back of the hand facing the target. The ring finger of the right hand is placed against the index finger of the left hand. The remaining fingers of the right hand are folded round the handle, with the little finger resting in the recess between the index and second fingers of the left hand. The thumb of the right hand is placed upon the top of the handle, which ensures that the palm of the right hand is facing the target. This used to be the most popular grip.

MUST KNOW

Good putting
This can ease the pressure on chipping and pitching and lead to more relaxed and successful play.

▼ Lay the grip of the putter across your left hand and then close the fingers round the shaft, with the thumb pointing down the centre of the club shaft.

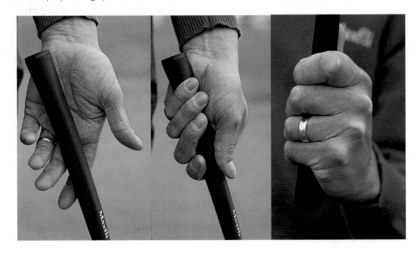

Building the grip

The correct way to build the overlapping grip is to lay the grip of the club across your left hand from a point at the first joint of the index finger through the palm into the butt of the hand. Close your fingers round the club shaft with the thumb pointing down the centre of the shaft. Place the palm of the right hand facing the hole, the little finger of the right hand overlapping the index finger of the left hand. The thumb of the right hand will be pointing down the shaft.

Golfers with small hands may find that when the little finger of the right hand overlaps the index finger of the left hand, it rests on top of the index finger. However, for people with long fingers, the little finger will rest in the cleft between the index finger and the third finger.

▲ A sideways view of the overlapping (Vardon) grip.

◀ Place the palm of the right hand facing the hole, the little finger of the right hand overlapping the index finger of the left hand. The thumb of the right hand will point down the shaft.

The interlocking grip

In this grip the left hand takes the same position as in the overlapping grip (see page 98), but, as the right hand closes around the handle, the little finger of the right hand interlocks with the index finger of the left hand, thereby interlocking the hands together.

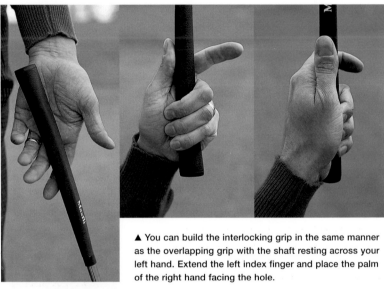

▲ You can build the interlocking grip in the same manner as the overlapping grip with the shaft resting across your left hand. Extend the left index finger and place the palm of the right hand facing the hole.

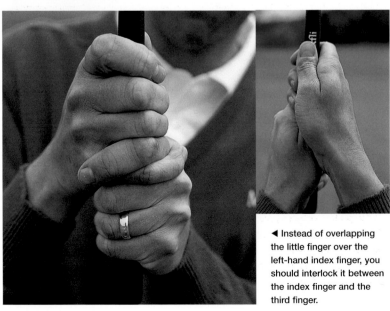

◄ Instead of overlapping the little finger over the left-hand index finger, you should interlock it between the index finger and the third finger.

The baseball grip

The two-handed baseball grip is sometimes preferred by golfers with very small hands or short fingers, particularly juniors and ladies. You should place the left hand on the handle of the club as in the overlapping grip. Grip the club with the left hand, then place all fingers of the right hand at

the bottom side of the handle with the fingers facing upwards, then apply similar pressure with all your fingers whilst closing the fingers and palm around the handle. Place the right thumb on top of the handle with the muscular base covering the left thumb.

▲ Build the grip in exactly the same way as before with the left hand, but note how all the fingers and thumbs must be on the club shaft with the hands close together.

MUST KNOW

Wrist action

The major problem with using all these conventional grips is that they tend to encourage overactive wrists which can lead to an inconsistent putting action. To try to avoid this, players have experimented with many variations, ranging from placing the index finger of one or both hands down the handle of the putter, to overlapping with two fingers of the right hand onto the left hand. Whatever grip you decide to adopt, a good touch can only be achieved with practice.

The reverse overlap grip

This has now become the most widely used of all the putting grips. What makes it so effective is that it minimizes wrist action by placing the handle more in the palms of both hands. This produces a more passive grip and permits the shoulder to initiate the pendulum action of the stroke.

▲ The reverse overlap grip.

▼ Start building the grip with the left hand index finger extended. The right-hand grip should also be as before but without any overlapping or interlocking. All the fingers of the right hand take up their natural position on the grip but the index finger of the left hand will overlap the first three fingers of the right hand.

Building the grip

To build the reverse overlap grip, start by placing the club handle diagonally across the heel pad of your left hand. Only the tips of the fingers should be on the grip; your left index finger will not be on the club, extending downwards and lying on the fingers of the right hand with your left thumb placed on the top of the handle running straight down. The handle rests at the base of the index finger of the right hand, with your right ring finger lying against the middle finger of your left hand.

The handle will run diagonally up across the palm towards a spot just under the heel pad. The club should not rest in your right palm. The fleshy part of your hand, just under the heel pad, should rest against the middle finger of your left hand. Your right thumb should be just to the left of the handle so it won't exert pressure and influence the putting stroke. The right hand will be turned slightly clockwise or under just a few degrees to maintain a relaxed position.

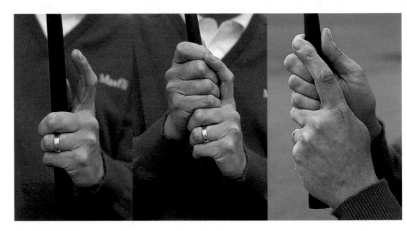

The two-finger reverse overlap grip

This is a variation on the normal reverse overlap grip (opposite). The main difference is that both the index fingers of the right and left hands will point straight down the club shaft instead of overlapping or interlocking. The fingers must be straight down the shaft and opposing each other. Take care not to move the fingers slightly across the shaft.

Which ever grip you decide to adopt, the most important consideration is to grip the putter in a way that binds the wrists to prevent either the right or left hand dominating as you putt. Most missed putts and badly judged distances are caused by last-minute hits with the right hand.

▲ If you use the two-finger reverse overlap grip, both your index fingers should point straight down the shaft.

Other grips

There are several other putting grips that are sometimes used but these are usually best avoided, especially by beginners to the game. They are used only when other more conventional putting methods have been tried and discarded due to people experiencing problems with them.

The split hands grip

This grip is very dangerous although it is used successfully by a few golfers. The angles across the back of the left hand and the palm of the right hand must be correct as in other grips – parallel to one another – or the hands will work against each other. This is not a solid grip, and it is not suitable for beginners and high-handicappers.

The side-saddle stance grip

This bizarre-looking technique is the croquet-style method of putting. Surprisingly, some golfers have found that it does work well for them and that it can even be very successful, especially if they have experienced problems with the more commonly used putting methods. However, it is seldom used by good putters and must be regarded only as a last resort.

The putting stroke

An efficient putting stroke will roll the ball across the green on the correct line and at the right speed for any distance. You must keep the ball rolling on the putting surface, not jumping up into the air or it is more likely to pull up short of the hole.

▲ The distance the ball travels is governed by the length of your stroke.

▶ For the pendulum stroke, the putter should meet the ball with its sole parallel to the ground (top left and right). Take care not to hit it too much on the upswing (below left) with your hands too far behind the putter head. Nor should you hit down on the ball too much (below right) with your hands too far in front of the putter face.

Pendulum putting

For a consistent feel for distance and line, contact the ball with the sole of the putter horizontal (parallel) to the ground. Avoid hitting the ball on a downward or upward approach, which will cause it to hop. Most good golfers use the pendulum putting stroke as it is easier to obtain level contact. The putter is kept level with the ball's equator for at least 23 cm (9 in) on either side of the ball, which is positioned just inside the left heel. The backswing and forward swing are equal in length.

This method is designed to minimize hand and wrist action with no breaking or hinging of the left wrist on the forward swing. Excessive wrist break and over-active hands may cause inconsistent ball contact and poor control of distance. This stroke promotes the feeling of a stroke, not a hit.

The set up

When you set up for a putt, you should stand comfortably over the ball, holding the putter lightly. Try to be relaxed and just focus on the line you want the ball to take. Bend forwards more from your hips than for your set up for other golf shots. If you were to drop a vertical line down from the front of your shoulders, it should fall a few inches in front of your toe line. However, do not put all your weight on your toes. Your weight should be distributed evenly between the balls of your feet and your heels.

Your do not have to keep your arms straight; each elbow can point inwards towards the corresponding hip bone. Do not press your arms hard against your body or you will not be able to keeping it still while your arms move. Try to hold your hands high, giving the wrists a better chance to remain firm throughout your stroke. The putter shaft is much closer to a vertical line than it is for a normal golf shot and therefore you will be standing much closer to the ball than usual. You will also find that the putter grip falls more into the palm of your left hand than for full shots.

▲ A good putting set up (top), with the eyes over the ball, the hands away from the legs, and the elbows pointing inwards towards the hips. The set up (above) shows the distance you would stand from the ball when hitting a full shot with an iron or similar club.

▲ A normal golf shot set up (above left). See how the grip on the club handle is different from the putting one (above right) and the arms are straighter and not so close to the body.

The grip and putter shaft

As we have seen, several putting grips can be used successfully for putting, but the reverse overlap grip (see page 102) is most common and has the best chance of success. The length of the putter you use is an important consideration.

● If the shaft is too long, it will cause you to stand up too straight with your arms too bent.

● If it is too short, you will crouch over too much and your arms will be too straight.

▲ Too long a putter shaft (above) will make your posture too upright and the eye line will not be over the ball; a short putter shaft will produce a crouched posture.

▶ Your hands should be held high (right) for the pendulum stroke. If they are too close to the body (far right), this will produce a wristy action.

Body alignment

For a normal straight putt, your feet and shoulder alignment should be parallel with the ball-to-hole line. Visualize a rectangle where the point at which your feet are aimed is equidistant from the hole, as your feet are from the ball.

▼ Your feet, knees, hips and shoulders should all point parallel to your target line. The ball to the right of the hole is the same distance from the hole as the player stands from the object ball.

Ball position

You can experiment with positioning the ball in different places in your stance but, ideally, it should be just inside the left heel and no further back than the centre. You want to contact the ball on a level approach, neither upwards nor downwards. Unlike other golf shots, your eye line should be directly over the ball. The easiest method of checking this is to get into your set-up position and then take a second ball and hold it between your eyes, on the bridge of your nose. Let it fall and it should land on top of the ball you are playing.

▲ This set up shows the correct position for the ball just inside the left heel.

◄ Hold a ball in your right hand on the bridge of your nose (far left) and then simply drop it (left). It should hit the ball on the ground if your eye line is over the ball.

MUST KNOW

The sweet spot

You must position the ball in line with the sweet spot on the putter blade or you will get a mishit and the ball will miss its target. You can find the sweet spot by holding the putter up in the air with two fingers at the grip end while tapping the putter face with your forefinger. When you tap the face and it swings without deviating or twisting, you have found the sweet spot where you must strike the ball.

The pendulum stroke

To produce the correct pendulum movement, you need to form a triangle of your arms and shoulders and which moves from a fulcrum at the back and base of your neck. Focus on keeping your legs, body and head very steady and feel your shoulders rocking back and forth.

MUST KNOW

Body weight

Your weight should be distributed slightly in favour of your left leg, approximately 60:40. As in all golf shots, the set up is of paramount importance and you cannot putt well from a bad address position.

Performing the pendulum

This movement is not the same as the full golf swing in which the shoulders turn around the trunk of the body. During the backswing, your right shoulder should move up slightly as your left shoulder moves down. On the follow through, the reverse happens – the left shoulder moves up and the right moves down. It is essential that

▲ You may swivel your head to have a final check along the putter line but do not lift it up or down and make sure you keep your body still.

Pre-stroke drills

Do not stand absolutely motionless for too long before you putt. To prevent yourself freezing over the ball, try the following:

- Tap the ground lightly just behind the ball before you start your stroke.
- Do not push down into the ground by resting your weight on the putter.
- Make small movements with your feet to get really settled.
- Press your hands forward towards the target, just prior to the take away.

the putter grip, shaft and head all move at the same pace and at a constant speed throughout. The length of your putting stroke will govern the distance that the ball will travel after impact.

▲ When striking the ball, imagine you are hitting the ball hard enough to roll just past the hole.

◄ The left shoulder has moved down, right shoulder up from the set up. The putter grip, shaft and head move at the same pace. The impact position is identical to address. The triangle and putter shaft relationship is maintained. The head, body and legs stay still.

Judging distance

Misjudging speed, especially on middle- and long-range putts, can lead to poor putting results and misjudged distance. How often have you been six feet short or six feet long on a putt? Even on a very badly directed line, you are unlikely to be more than two or three feet off line.

Developing a feel for distance

The advantage of the pendulum putting stroke is that it is generally more reliable in promoting a better feel for distance than a hitting action. The backswing and follow through correspond in length, like the movement of a clock pendulum.

Do not make the mistake of using the same length of stroke to hit the ball, no matter what the distance, but try to hit it harder or softer. This leads to excessive hand action so always ensure that the backswing is sufficiently long to permit gradual acceleration without having to speed it up with your hands. Try to think of the ball as if it just happens to be in the way of the putter head as it moves smoothly through the middle part of the stroke rather than hitting at it consciously.

▲ Longer putts require a longer backswing and through swing. You do not have to hit the ball harder.

▲ Place a tee 30 cm (12 in) on either side of the ball to help develop a backswing and follow through which are of equal length.

Distance swing drill

Practise your stroke without aiming at a target. Take six balls on to the putting green and then make pendulum strokes of varying lengths:
- Two balls with a 15-cm (6-in) backswing and through swing.
- Two with a 30-cm (12-in) swing.
- Two with a 45-cm (18-in) movement, and so on.

Keep the pace of your stroke constant, focusing on a consistent strike, and notice how the roll distance varies according to the stroke length. Place a tee in the ground 30 cm (12 in) behind the ball and another tee 30 cm (12 in) after the ball. Position it about an inch outside your intended target line. This exercise will provide a simple visual guide to the length of your stroke on either side of the ball.

▲ Put into practice the distance swing drill by putting from three different distances. You can judge the overall distance of a long putt more easily if you get into the good habit of breaking the putt down into several smaller distances.

▲ The channel created by the tees on the ground shows how the putter head swing should remain parallel to the target line.

Direction

The ball's direction is influenced by your aim, the face of your putter at impact, and the swing line that the putter head moves along on either side of the ball. The arc followed by the head is less pronounced than for a full swing. On short putts, there should be no curve in the swing and the putter should move on a straight line through the ball. On longer putts the swing will curve slightly inside on the backswing and follow through.

MUST KNOW

Putting for distance and direction
Always remember the following points:
- The putter face must aim at your target – the hole – for a straight putt.
- Your feet and body line should aim slightly left.
- Your shoulders, arms, hands and putter shaft should all move together as one unit.
- Your legs, body and head should stay still.
- The backswing and forward swing should always be of equal length.
- The pace of the pendulum putting stroke should stay constant throughout.

Practise your putting

As your stroke becomes more consistent, you can practise putting at varying distances from the hole. This will help you to develop a feel for how long a stroke you need to roll the ball for different distances. You must remember, however, that a five-foot putt on a slow green will require a longer stroke than a putt of the same distance on a faster green.

▼ Slide the putter handle inside the cuff (below left) and grip lower down the club as you take your normal pendulum stroke. Keep the end of the putter grip against the inside of the left forearm as you putt (centre) to help promote the feel of the pendulum. Do not do this drill off the practice green.

The cuff drill

For this drill on the practice green, you must wear a sweater with a tight wrist cuff. Slide the top of the putter shaft inside your left sleeve and then take your normal putting grip with your right hand just onto the chrome of the shaft. The putter grip should remain against the inside of your left forearm throughout the stroke. This practice routine will help promote the pendulum feeling.

The long-shafted putter

Some tour pros use a specially adapted practice putter with a shaft that is 30–37 cm (12–15 in) longer than standard. Hold the grip at normal length so the shaft extension rests along the inside of the left forearm to a point above the elbow. This helps promote the feeling of the arms and putter shaft moving together.

Lining up putts

To line up your putts successfully, you will need to develop your skills of concentration and visualization. One way of achieving this is to work hard on your practice drills on the putting green. To putt consistently well, you not only need a sound stroke but also the ability to read the green and see in your mind's eye all the different variables that can affect any specific putt.

Putting tip
When putting, align the manufacturer's name on the ball to the line you are going to take, not the hole.

◄ On the practice green try holing a variety of putts with balls at different distances from the hole. You could try the clock method whereby you hit from around the hole as on a clock face.

Left-handed putting drill

Putting with your left hand (if you are right-handed) will train your left side so you use your left hand, wrist, arm and shoulder correctly. With your right hand on your right thigh and shoulders square to the target line, putt a few balls with your left hand only. If you are doing it right, your club face should be square to the target line and the balls will cluster.

▲ If the balls do not cluster together, your left wrist is hinging on the forward swing.

Putting conditions

You will not always have the pleasure of putting on perfect greens in warm, sunny conditions and you will notice that, as the seasons change, the putting conditions will be affected and you will have to adapt your putting technique accordingly. It is essential to understand how putting greens react to different weather conditions and how the normal seasonal greenkeeping practices can affect the playing characteristics of the greens. You must allow for these in your game.

Playing in the rain

Rain slows down the speed of the putting surface as it takes time for water to drain away and the green to recover and regain its pace. Inland greens on heavy clay-type soil will recover their original speed more slowly than sand-based seaside greens. After prolonged rain, similar greens on the same course may have varying characteristics. Steeply banked greens or greens in hollows may attract more water, as will undulating surfaces, and will recover more slowly. High and low levels on the same green will recover at different rates.

▲ In wet weather, always make a point of cleaning your putter before and after taking a stroke.

▶ Sunny weather just after a heavy thunderstorm can make the green conditions change rapidly. The green in the foreground is flat and exposed to the elements, especially the wind, which can dry a green extremely quickly. The green in the backgound is protected by trees and therefore will tend to have a slower pace than the green in front of it.

Playing in heat and frost

In long spells of hot, sunny weather, the ground will harden and thus the pace of the putting surface will become significantly faster. However, putting on frosty greens in the winter is more a matter of luck than skill. The ground will be quite compacted so you must remember to allow for a quicker speed and a greater break. As the temperature rises and the frost thaws, the rolling ball will gather ice and water, thereby slowing it down and reducing break.

Green location

Greens that are located in dense trees or nestling down in hollows can produce problems for the golfer. A green which is enclosed by trees that block out the sunlight will obviously take longer to recover from rain and frost, and fallen leaves from the trees may also be troublesome, especially in the autumn. Greens in hollows may have a slower rate of recovery from frost, and steep banking around these green may create a run of water on to the surface after rainfall. When you are playing a round out on the course, you should be aware of these seasonal and varying playing conditions.

Putting tip
Before the greens can dry out, natural drainage must occur, but strong winds and high temperatures can accelerate this drying process. In dry conditions, automatic watering during the day will slow down putting speed and reduce the break on the greens.

▼ Seaside links greens with sand-based soil are more exposed to the wind and will dry out rapidly. They are nearly always faster than clay-based inland courses.

Grass and its influence on your stroke

Different grass types on greens will affect the way in which you putt. Most greens are composed of a coarse, broad-leaf meadow grass creating a slower surface, but many new courses have introduced creeping bent grasses, a fine narrow-leaf grass which produces a quick putting surface with greater break. Seaside links courses often tend to have bents and fescue grasses which are generally quicker surfaces.

MUST KNOW

Learn the terms
● Borrow refers to the margin of distance the ball should be played to the left or right of the hole.
● Break is the extent to which the ball leaves your intended line for a specific putt.

▼ The grass on this green is a very fine fescue, an ideal putting surface for fast-pace greens. It tends to be faster than the coarser broad-leaf meadow grass on some courses.

The role of the greenkeeper

There is a perceptible change in the speed of the green after it has been cut, and it is the greenkeeper's job is to create the best possible putting surface, depending on the weather and seasonal variations. The height of cut of the grass will affect your feel and judgement. As a general rule, the height of cut is greater in spring and autumn, thereby slowing down putting speed and break.

It is usually lower in summer to produce faster surfaces and greater break. The grass does not grow during the cold winter months and it may thin out so the speed of the greens may vary. Top dressing and verti-cutting will also create faster putting surfaces so it may be worth checking whether these practices are carried out at your local course.

▶ The lines on this green denote that it has been cut by hand.

How to read break

You will learn how to visualize a straight line to the hole, but reading break is more difficult. There are so many factors that can affect the way in which a ball reacts to the contours on a green. To read break successfully, you must evaluate the green conditions and determine the strength and speed of stroke you need to achieve the curvature to the hole.

Calculate the break

Crouch down behind the ball. Try and visualize how it will curve and break. Get a mental picture of the ball rolling on a straight line towards the hole. This will help you to calculate at what point, and by how much, it will break from this line.

Practice drill

Choose a six-foot putt on a sloping section of a putting green, then place four balls around the hole in positions with a different break. Get down 10 feet behind the ball with your eye-line as low as possible. Visualize a straight line to the hole and then try to work out the amount of borrow needed.

The grain of the grass

The grain will affect the speed and break of a putt, especially where a coarse grass is sown, usually in hot climates. If you are putting down-grain, where the blades of grass lean towards the hole, the ball will tend to run faster; if the grain is towards you, the speed of the ball will be slower.

On a straight putt, where the grain runs across the line, you may need to aim outside the hole. Where the grain runs in the opposite direction, on a left-to-right or right-to-left break, you must decide how it could affect the break and then judge the margin you borrow. Straight putts with the grain tend to be very fast but putts against the grain are much slower. A good tip is that if the grass is shiny and lying flat and away from you, there is a down grain. Conversely, if the grass is dull and against you, there is an up grain.

▲ The three tee pegs on the left indicate the slope and the break. In between the second and third tee pegs is the point of break.

want to know **more?**

Take it to the next level...

Go to...
- ▶ **Chipping and pitching** – page 118
- ▶ **Playing a round** – page 132
- ▶ **Golf rules and etiquette** – page 185

Other sources
- ▶ **Your local golf professional**
  for professional putting instruction
- ▶ **Videos and DVDs**
  for putting instruction
- ▶ **Internet**
  for interactive CD-ROMs
- ▶ **Golf schools**
  for specialist putting tuition
- ▶ **Publications**
  visit www.collins.co.uk for Collins golf books

chipping

& pitching

An effective short game can
make all the difference between
winning or losing a match.
Although not as glamorous as
the long game, it is well worth
perfecting it if you want to lower
your handicap. Don't waste
your practice sessions just
thrashing away with your driver;
concentrate on your wedge
and putter and watch those
scores come tumbling down.

Chipping

One of the simplest yet most important shots in golf is the chip from the fringe of the green. Many golfers make this stroke look complicated, but, if played correctly, it really is simple and can be a saviour in helping to lower your scores. Play this shot with a pitching wedge or 7 iron. With practice, you will soon be able to judge the amount of carry and run.

▲ The secret of playing a successful chip shot is to judge how the ball will react on landing. Keep your left wrist firm through the hitting area with the club face facing your intended target.

The set up

You use the same technique, whichever club you employ (your wedge or 7 iron), except that for the same length of shot the more lofted wedge needs to be struck more firmly because of the greater backspin it creates.

In the address position for this shot, you should open your stance a little but no more than feels comfortable and natural. This will enable you to judge the line and length more accurately than from a squarer position. Place the ball back in your stance nearer the right foot. Hold the club towards the bottom of the grip (an inch or two nearer the shaft) for extra

MUST KNOW

Chipping from the rough

A chip shot from the rough by the side of the green will run further than one played from shorter grass on the apron of the green. The longer grass between the club head and ball will reduce the backspin. When you set up for this shot, position the ball more towards the right foot and open the club face a fraction. Use a wedge for this shot and accelerate through the ball with an outside-to-in swing line. The wrists should cock earlier on the backswing in order to create a steeper takeaway and a sharper descending arc into the ball.

control, and stand close to the ball with your arms close to your body. Shift most of your weight on to your left foot and place your hands well in front of the club head so that the shaft slopes towards the target.

▲ The set up for a simple running chip with a 7 iron. Note the comfortable, open stance which makes it easy to judge both the distance and direction.

Playing the shot

To play the chip shot successfully, keep the club head low to the ground throughout the swing, allowing the wrists to break only slightly in the backswing with your weight remaining on the left side. Make a smooth, unhurried brushing stroke through the ball with the hands leading all the way. This shot is not unlike a long putt with a more lofted club in which you allow the loft on the club face to carry the ball through the air for the short distance necessary.

Avoiding common faults

Try to avoid the most common faults which are:
- A bad set up with the ball too far forward and the hands and weight too far back.
- 'Scooping' the ball into the air using too much wrist action.
- Leaning back on the right foot.

If you tend to hit poor chip shots, one of these faults may be causing the problem. So try to analyze where you are going wrong and which of the above applies to you. Practise your chipping and you will soon be able to roll three shots into two around the greens on a regular basis. Keep it simple and it will help you to reduce your handicap.

▶ Notice how the hands lead the club face through impact and all the way through to the completion of the swing – there is no flicking of the wrists. You must allow the loft on the club face to lift the ball slightly. If you make the backswing purely with your hands, the right hand will try to scoop the ball up on the upswing and this will result in a poor shot.

Pitching

Another useful shot to have in your repertory is the short, fairly high pitch. It looks so easy when the tour pros put the ball next to the flag yet many beginners have problems with this shot. The swing for the pitch is just the full swing in miniature but judging distance accurately is essential.

The set up

Many people who can play a full shot and can cope with a simple chip from just off the edge of the green regard the pitch as a 'clever half shot' which is best left to the experts. However, the pitch is, after a putt, the most commonly played shot in golf and it is well worth mastering if you want to reduce your handicap.

For a pitch shot, you should make some minor modifications to your normal set up. Position the ball in the centre of your stance with your hands ahead of the ball. Your weight should be fractionally more on the left side than usual. Addressing the ball in this way will help produce a sharper downswing into the ball and impart more backspin.

The swing

Basically, you need the same swing as for a full wedge shot but, because you are not hitting the the ball so far, less of it. If a full wedge flies 90 yards, you should aim to take half as much swing for a pitch of 45 yards. It is essential that you strike the ball with a smoothly accelerating club head. Think of the relationship between length of swing and length of shot in terms of a clock face. If your backswing reaches 10 o'clock, your follow through should finish at 2 o'clock. If your backswing goes to 8 o'clock then the follow through should stop at 4 o'clock. Your stance will become narrower and progressively

Don't fluff!

Many beginners playing a pitch shot make the common mistake of leaning back on to the right foot in an attempt to scoop the ball high into the air, but this will usually result in a fluffed or thinned shot. Try to trust your swing and allow the loft on your club to do the work and create the shot for which it was designed.

◄ When pitching, the same principles apply as for any other golf shot. On this shot of 60 yards, your hands will reach 10 o'clock on the backswing and will then swing through to finish at about 2 o'clock.

MUST KNOW

A ball in its own pitch mark

If the ball is deeply embedded in its own pitch mark in the sand you must change your technique.

1 Position the ball opposite the right foot and use a very steep backswing, straight back from the ball in line with the target.

2 Hit firmly down into the sand 7–10 cm (3–4 in) behind the ball and do not try to follow through. The ball will blast out much lower than normal, with very little backspin, and will run a long way.

▼ This pitch shot travelled about 35 yards. The hands swung back to the 8 o'clock position on the backswing and round to 4 o'clock at the finish. The movements of the legs and upper body are a smaller version of a full golf swing.

more open for shorter shots. You must strike the ball positively and slightly on the downswing so that the grooves on the club face bite into its surface and produce backspin. The loft on your club will lift the ball into the air so keep your club face square through impact and into the follow through to create maximum backspin.

Practise your pitching

The pitch is a useful shot to play when you need more height on the ball – for example, lofting the ball over a greenside bunker. Never neglect your pitching clubs in practice sessions – they will repay you with better shots as well as lower scores so work on mastering this shot.

Practise hitting different lengths of bunker shot (see page 128), resisting the temptation to vary the distance that you hit behind the ball. Just adjust the length of your swing, as you would for a pitch from grass. Nor should you attempt to scoop the ball out of a bunker, even when it is close to the lip and needs to rise steeply. Instead, make your stance a little more open with the ball positioned further forward and trust your swing. From this position, you can make the ball rise almost vertically.

▲ This is the swing you should use for all but the most unusual shots from bunkers. It should be smooth, unhurried and rhythmic. Do not be tempted to force your swing but focus instead on swinging the club head down into the sand and through to the target without rushing.

Pitching out of a bunker

For a standard bunker shot, always use a sand iron, which is designed specifically for this job, and don't try to pull off miracles – just play within your limitations. If the shot seems too difficult to attempt, don't automatically aim for the flag. Take a penalty drop into an easier position within the bunker and then get out on to the green. It's not worth dropping more shots by trying to pull off heroic recoveries. Nor should you try to lift the ball cleanly off the sand – this is one of the most difficult shots in the game.

If you are unlucky and your ball lands in a bunker, don't panic and don't attempt to lean backwards and lift the ball up and out. Just practise the method described and you will overcome your fear and become a proficient and confident bunker player.

▲ Play the shot like a normal pitch but with maximum backswing to get the ball as close as possible to the pin.

Don't lift

You must not try to lift a ball over a bunker; just swing firmly and smoothly down and through the ball. Your sand wedge has a loft of between 52 and 60 degrees – more than enough to generate both the height and backspin you need.

Pitching over bunkers

This shot often strikes fear into the average golfer who instinctively feels the need to hit the ball with a high, gentle flight in order to stop it quickly. However, most bunkers do not have a high lip and all you need to do is carry the ball past them. Ignore the sand and pick out a spot on the green as your landing area. Using the most lofted club in your bag, swing at the ball smoothly and strike it crisply forward and down. Keep the weight more on the left side than usual to encourage the contact you are seeking.

You are looking for backspin, not height, so trust your swing and the loft on your club to produce the shot you want. Never try to lift the ball into the air, which is a recipe for disaster. This stroke requires the maximum amount of backswing in order to hit the ball near to the pin. Use a sand iron to make use of its great loft and play the shot like any other pitch.

want to know **more?**

Take it to the next level...

Go to...
- ▶ **Playing a round** – page 132
- ▶ **Overcoming hazards** – page 64
- ▶ **Golf rules and etiquette** – page 183

Other sources
- ▶ **Your local golf professional**
  for pitching and chipping lessons
- ▶ **Videos and DVDs**
  for short game tuition
- ▶ **Internet**
  interactive CD-ROMs
- ▶ **Magazines**
  for specialist features
- ▶ **Publications**
  visit www.collins.co.uk for Collins golf books

a round

To play a round of golf, you must be prepared mentally and physically. Plan your round in advance, working out your strategy while playing within your limitations. Take it hole by hole; focus on the one you are playing and don't worry about hazards on the next one. When your round is over, try to analyze your game and learn from your mistakes.

Practise before you play

Before you engage in any sport, you should always stretch and loosen up physically as well as compose your mind and focus yourself mentally. You will not play a good round and end up with a low score if you arrive late, grab your golf bag and then dash straight on to the first tee. Always try to arrive at the course with plenty of time to spare. If you get there at least 30 minutes early, then you can use this time profitably to prepare yourself on the practice ground.

MUST KNOW

Be confident
Building up your confidence in your ability to play well through regular practice will bring enormous benefits to your game and will improve your chances of reproducing your good practice shots out on the course in competition.

Advantages of practice

These are myriad. Not only does practice build confidence as you improve and expand your repertoire of shots but it also imposes a useful mental and physical discipline. You can groove a swing if you repeat it often enough so that it becomes an automatic part of your muscle memory. The more you practise, the quicker your muscles will remember how they function and interact. This will result not only in stronger muscles but it will also promote a powerful,

▶ Allow some time before a game to hit some practice shots. Hitting some balls into an open umbrella will help to get you in the mood and develop your feel.

energy-efficient swing, taking some of the tension out of your game and helping you relax.

If you have hit the same shot hundreds of times on the practice ground you will be more confident of playing it well in a match when it really matters. There is an old golfing adage that golf is played in the smallest area of any sport: in the few inches between your ears! Practising your shots will improve your game and make you more confident of what is achievable.

Relax into your game

Warm up gradually by hitting a few shots. Start with some wedge shots and work up slowly until you are hitting some balls with your driver. Just relax and swing in a smooth, unhurried way, enjoying your golf and settling into a rhythm. Do not neglect your short game; practise some putts of varying lengths on the putting green.

Take this opportunity to try to judge the speed of the greens and assess the pace. Use this time to get a feel for your putter and the condition of the greens before you play a real round. Remember that you are just practising and preparing yourself so relax into your golfing routines and get into the right frame of mind to play well out on the course.

▲ When you arrive at the golf course, head for the practice ground and spend some time hitting a few shots or practising some putting before you proceed to the first tee.

MUST KNOW

Loosen up

As well as warming up with some golf shots on the practice ground, you will need to loosen up your golfing muscles. It is always a good idea to perform some simple stretching routines before hitting the ball in earnest. For a complete guide to all the exercises you can perform, including those for improving your posture, strength and endurance, turn to page 136.

Warm-up exercises

Always warm up before you play golf. You should never go straight to the tee and hit the first ball in earnest without performing some loosening movements to stretch out your muscles gently. Ideally, you should allow yourself time to hit 20 or so practice balls before playing, starting with some short wedge or 9-iron shots and working up to the long clubs to finish with a few drives. However, if time prohibits this, try and use these warm-up exercises to help get your golfing muscles ready for action.

Club behind your back

Hold a club behind your back between your elbows (as shown in the photographs, right) and then pivot your body to mimic the way it turns in the golf swing. First, turn your hips and shoulders to the right through 90 degrees as on the backswing, then 90 degrees to the left on the follow through. This will stretch out your muscles as you simulate the action of the swing.

Shoulder exercise

An alternative is to hold a club shaft across your shoulders by crossing your forearms and pressing the shaft against your shoulders. Push the right shoulder back with your left hand until the shaft line has turned through 90 degrees. Keep your head steady. Turn your shoulders in the opposite direction so your hips, right knee and foot move across to the left. Feel the weight transference on to your right leg on the backswing turn, and your left leg on the follow through.

▶ This simple warm-up exercise is relaxing and not too strenuous. Hold the club behind your elbows and turn 90 degrees to the right and then 90 degrees to the left to mimic the golf swing.

Two-club swing

This is a good way to loosen up and release any tension in your body. Hold the end of the grip of a golf club in each hand and swing them slowly and loosely backwards and forwards. Start with short swings and then gradually lengthen them until you are at full stretch. The purpose of this simple warm-up exercise is to loosen up your arms and wrists before you venture out on to the course and make a full golf swing.

▲ Swinging two golf clubs slowly backwards and forwards in front of you and then behind you will loosen up your arms and wrists in readiness for your first swing.

MUST KNOW

Posture reminder
- Hold a golf club at the head end with your right hand, standing erect.
- With your hand behind your shoulder, hold the club shaft against your back from the base of your spine to the back of your head.
- Then bend forwards slowly from the hips, keeping the club shaft against your spine with your chin up and your left arm hanging freely away from your body. This spine angle is one of the most important factors in the set up and will influence the way in which you swing.

PLAYING A ROUND

137

▲ With knees slightly bent, bring both arms forward at shoulder height and round the spine with your head down to feel a stretch at the back of the shoulders. Hold for 6 seconds, then release.

▲ Strong thighs provide a stable base for your swing. With legs shoulder distance apart, squat down as if you were skiing. Hold and bounce gently up and down. Lift one heel off the ground, then the other until your thighs rebel and muscles start shaking.

Golf fitness exercises

There are three elements that you can develop to improve your golf: strength, flexibility and muscular endurance.

● Strength is essential for producing distance.

● Strength must be allied to a supple, flexible body in order to reach the positions that allow for full use of the muscular strength available.

● Muscular endurance means that the muscles can still perform efficiently even after many holes of golf, while a healthy heart and lungs will help prevent you tiring easily.

Gender and age

Many men tend to lose their flexibility as they get older thereby restricting their ability to turn fully on the swing. This results in a loss of power. Women do become less flexible as they age, but lack of strength is the factor that most restricts their club head speed and, thereby, distance.

Build a fitness programme

Assess your strengths and weaknesses to decide which exercises will benefit you most. You should concentrate on your hands, forearms, trunk rotation, back, abdomen and legs. The golf swing is a rotary movement, so any exercise that emphasizes the rotation of the trunk is very

---

MUST KNOW

Strengthen your hands and wrists

Strength in your fingers, hands and wrists will help you to control the golf club. Use a grip squeezer, especially in your left hand (because most right-handed players are much weaker in their left hands). This is one of the best and easiest ways to improve these important golf muscles. Equal strength in each hand is ideal, but not often found.

◀ Lift your right arm and extend it down behind your shoulder. Place your left hand on your bent right elbow and push down gently until you feel the stretch in your upper arm. Repeat the exercise with the other arm.

◀ With your legs crossed, lean over from your waist as far as you can towards your toes. Hold for 6 seconds; feel the stretch in your hamstrings. Repeat on the other side.

beneficial. For most people, just a few minutes a day spent practising some of the suggested exercises would help considerably in toning their bodies as well as gently and gradually increasing their strength. If practised regularly, they will benefit your health and your golf game. However, do not overdo it and wear yourself out. Build a programme that trains, not strains. For example, five of these exercises repeated 10 times each would be enough for most people initially. Increase or decrease the number of repetitions according to what feels comfortable for you.

▲ Stand up straight with both your arms extended behind you and hands clasped. Push back until you feel the stretch in your arms and shoulders. Hold for 6 seconds, then release.

Plan your shots

It is beneficial for any golfer, whether you are a humble novice or a tour pro, to plan out your shots. Any professional would be able to give you a detailed description of the type and shape of shot they planned to take, and its exact landing area.

Course strategy

Like the professionals, plan out what you intend to do and visualize your perfect shot. If you watch the top pros, they appear to swing on auto pilot, confident that their well-grooved swings will produce the desired shots. You can learn from their example: if you have a clear objective and plan accordingly, you have a better chance of succeeding and hitting a good shot.

▲ Whether it is a simple putt or a match-winning drive, always take time to visualize your shot first.

Plan each hole

Everyone should learn about course management and strategy. As your skill level improves, you can adjust your strategy accordingly. If you plan to play a hole in a specific way, you are more likely to achieve good shots rather than simply aiming straight and adopting the 'hit and hope for the best' approach.

▼ On a par 3 hole like this one, aim for the left side of the green which allows a greater margin for error. Do not try to pull off the shot of a lifetime and go for the pin.

Good planning is important and you will soon learn that a straightforward attack on a hole is not always the easiest way to reach your goal. If you know approximately how far you are likely to hit the ball with each club and what kind of shot you most often produce, you can begin to formulate your own strategy for each hole and, hopefully, lower your scores in the process.

Know your limitations

Many beginners make the mistake of playing in a way that is beyond their capabilities. Don't go for a brilliant recovery shot only to fail and find yourself in deeper trouble. The best way to escape from trouble following a poor shot is to take the easiest and quickest route back to the fairway.

So how do you know what your limitations are? You should know how far you are likely to hit the ball with any given club. If you don't, take a bag of balls on to the practice ground and hit some with various clubs, measuring the distance to your average shot with each one. Armed with this information, you can tackle a shot over a hazard with more calculation than guesswork.

▼ As a beginner, you are unlikely to score many threes during your round so the par 3 holes are your best bet. You may be tempted to go recklessly for the pin but this strategy seldom pays off. On the hole shown here, you should aim for the left half of the green where even a poor shot will leave a chance of a three. Only in a desperate situation in matchplay should you consider going directly for the pin since there is almost no margin for error.

▲ Know your limitations and you can plan for a realistic shot rather than a miracle.

Alternatively, if your ball sometimes ends up surrounded by trees after an errant tee-shot, attempting to hit it through a distant, narrow gap is not a sensible option. How are you going to achieve a difficult shot like this if you miss the fairway even when the ball is sitting up nicely on a peg on the tee? Defensive golf is usually best but not always so. If you have a good chance of success, go for the shot, but not if the odds are stacked against you. Be realistic and only do what you can reasonably expect to accomplish.

Lower your scores

Although most of us play golf for the fun of it and because we enjoy the ultimate challenge of pitting ourselves against the course, we will not be happy unless our good shots are reflected in our overall score. Putting yourself under pressure to produce a good end result may well affect how you play during your round. It is impossible to focus fully on the shot in hand if you are forever worrying about the state of your score when compared with your handicap or par.

One shot at a time

Like your golfing heroes playing on the Tour, you need to develop the ability to play just one shot at a time – this can make all the difference between producing good and bad play. Even for a beginner, failing to forget an earlier missed putt or a bad bounce into the rough or a bunker and then brooding over it as you move on to other holes around the golf course can seriously affect your concentration on the shot in hand.

Thinking in terms of your overall progress in scoring is counter-productive, so learn to play each shot or hole separately. Don't even consider your score for the round until you have hit your last shot on the eighteenth green, and don't waste valuable energy worrying or comparing your efforts to those

MUST KNOW

Stroke by stroke
Relax and soak up the atmosphere, enjoy the company of your fellow golfers and remember that a golf score is made up from numerous strokes which are all of identical value. Play stroke by stroke and hole by hole to build your score.

in previous games. The better you are able to keep the 18 holes separate, the more successful you will be at achieving good scores and lowering your handicap. From your very earliest rounds of golf, you should concentrate on viewing each hole as a separate entity. If you learn to do this, the quicker you will improve. Initially, you may not find it easy as it is natural to analyze your game and how you are progressing along the way, but try to focus on the hole in hand and this attitude will reap dividends and will lead to lower scores.

Empty your mind

Most of the time you spend playing golf is taken up not by hitting the ball, which accounts for only a few minutes in an average round lasting about four hours, but by walking after it or searching for it. This interval between shots is very important to your mind set. If you become obsessive about scoring, the pressure to perform well may be overwhelming and your game could collapse as a result. Instead, try to empty your mind after each shot and just enjoy the surroundings and the whole experience of being out in the fresh air in a beautiful place.

▲ Keep focused on the hole you are playing and plan your shot carefully. Banish all other thoughts of past and future holes from your mind and concentrate on your desired shot.

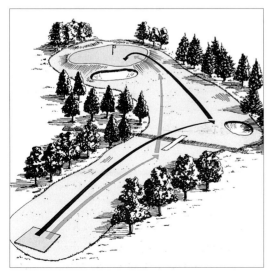

◀ There are two ways to play this hole; the black route is used by a pro or a low-handicap player, but you could try this if you are confident of clearing the ditch with your tee-shot. If this were an early hole in the round when you are not fully loosened up, or later if your swing is not as good as it should be, the second route might be preferable. Playing up short of the ditch and green leaves an easy pitch to the flag, giving you a chance of a four; if not, an almost certain five.

Par

All golf holes have a nominated value of 3, 4 and 5 – known as par. Par is determined by the length of a hole:

- Par 3: holes of 250 yards and under.
- Par 4: holes from 251 to 475 yards inclusive.
- Par 5: holes of 476 yards and over.

Par and handicap

The length of a hole is the most significant factor in determining its par value, but the degree of difficulty is also relevant. Thus, a long par 4 could be just below the required distance but, if it played steeply uphill, it could be termed a par 5. Similarly, if a hole had a water feature in front of the green, making it unlikely that most golfers could reach the green with their second shots, it could be allocated a par of 5.

The handicapping system

Based on a player's score in relation to the par of the course, this method measures your ability. Players of widely differing abilities can compete with each other on equal terms, but because each hole has a predetermined value (par), you may feel under pressure to play that hole to a preset standard. Par is defined mainly by distance but not all golfers hit the ball the same way so shorter hitters may be tempted to swing harder than they should. If this applies to you, work out the par on each hole based on your personal ability in terms of achievable distance.

▶ This long par 5 shows two distinct routes to the hole: a typically bunkered approach taken by some very good golfers, and a less direct, but far more sensible, approach. By taking the direct route you risk going into the fairway bunker and leave yourself with a testing third shot to the pin. Playing into the wide areas of the fairway would not only be safer but would also offer a much easier pitch – more likely to earn the par you seek.

For instance, the par of a hole of 470 yards may be 4 but most high handicappers would struggle to reach the green in two shots. However, if the hole is viewed as a par 5, you can approach it in a more relaxed way, allowing yourself three shots to reach the green. Working out the course in this way will give you a much higher total par figure but it is a more realistic standard by which you can judge your performance. As you become more experienced and skillful, you can lower your personal par for the course. This enables you to measure your improvement while avoiding the danger of trying too hard and too soon to achieve an unrealistic target.

Weigh up the odds

In spite of good planning, golf balls will still find a way to miss the fairway or green and will end up in the rough, trees or hazards and you will be faced with a recovery shot. It is best to accept that you have dropped a stroke and take the shortest, safest route possible back to the short grass.

If you opt for a 'make or break' stroke, consider why you are in this situation – your failure to hit a successful shot from a good lie on the fairway or a perfect one on the tee. So how can you expect to achieve a perfect recovery shot from a less than perfect lie in the rough? If you find yourself in trouble, weigh up the odds on success or failure. If those odds are favourable, consider playing the risky shot but only if you are confident.

Damage limitation is the name of the game so do what is necessary to get back onto the short grass without throwing away too many shots and taking unnecessary risks. This approach will pay dividends in the long term.

◀ This is a typical par 4 with an opportunity for a spectacular drive across the corner of the dog leg leaving a shorter second shot to the green. The odds on pulling this off are high. Common sense dictates you take a shorter club from the tee towards the fairway bunker and well away from the trees. This opens up the green for your second shot which should be aimed into the wide central area so you don't have to play over the greenside trap.

The mind game

How often have you heard it said that golf is a game of inches? After all, a two-inch putt has the same value as a 300-yard drive. However, the most important inches are those between your ears, and it does not matter how good your technique is if your mental attitude is not conducive to playing well. If your mental state is not perfect, you cannot expect your body to produce a successful shot.

Stay in control

To play a good round of golf, you should be calm and controlled like the top pros. Getting excited in anticipation of a good round may not bring the results you seek, nor will being too hard on yourself and wallowing in self pity when things go wrong. If you always approach your golf in a mood of quiet determination and calm, ready to accept whatever comes and focusing on one shot at a time, you will enjoy your round more and lower your scores.

▼ Focus solely on the shot you are playing and work out your strategy in advance. Stay calm and don't be intimidated by any hazards.

Boost your concentration

Being calm is very beneficial but you do need to concentrate fully on each shot. If it is intrinsically interesting, it is easier to become absorbed and to focus your attention on it to the exclusion of all else. However, as an average round takes between three and four-and-a-half hours, it is difficult to maintain a high level of concentration for that length of time. But remember that very little of the total time out on the course is actually spent hitting the ball – only three to four minutes. Concentrating only for that short time is not too taxing.

Don't waste your time when walking between shots – relax and enjoy the social elements of golf. You can start thinking about your next shot as you approach the ball. Try to keep your mind on what is happening right now, not what caused that last bad hole. Equally, don't worry about later holes on the course that you have not reached yet. As you approach your ball, take note of anything that might affect your next stroke. Check the lie and target area; and

▲ When you are walking between shots, try to relax and chat to your playing partner. Don't start worrying about your next shot until you get to your ball.

▼ Clear your mind of all other thoughts when you are planning your shot and preparing to hit the ball. Make sure you focus totally on the job in hand.

calculate how the weather may affect the flight of the ball. By focusing exclusively on these things, by the time you are ready to swing, you are concentrating totally on the job in hand.

Once you have hit the ball, you cannot alter its path, so relax and turn your mind to other things. Learning to switch on and off in this way ensures that your brain does not become overloaded and that your interest in each shot is maintained. This is easier and less stressful than trying to concentrate for several hours at a stretch.

Positive is best

Most people are optimistic by nature and a single positive thought is more beneficial than a series of negative instructions issued from your brain to your body. For instance, how many times have you been told in golf not to move your head? This is a negative command which distracts your attention from where it should be: on the club head and the ball. Instead, it is better to suggest that you watch the club strike the ball, as this is a simple positive command which will focus your mind on the correct area.

▲ Don't be put off by the challenges a course may throw at you. Just play one hole at a time and enjoy the beautiful scenery as you walk between the holes.

MUST KNOW

Be positive
If you hit a poor shot, don't look for all the reasons why you might have failed but try to form a strong visual image of your swing and keep those swing thoughts simple and positive.

Build a routine

When we watch the top pros on television or go along to a tournament, we have a wonderful opportunity to learn from the best exponents of golf. However, instead of studying their individual swing techniques, look at the way in which they conduct themselves and how they approach each shot.

A pre-shot routine

The stars have developed their own pre-shot routines which they perform before hitting the ball. For instance, they might always approach the ball from the same angle or take the same number of waggles. In other words, they have found their own ideal preparation for a shot and consciously repeated the movement until it is automatic.

Develop your own routine to help you cope with pressure during a round. It will make you feel more secure; familiarity breeds comfort and confidence. By slipping into your never-changing pre-shot routine, you won't rush a stroke or try too hard. Find out what works best for you and then stick with it. It will become an integral part of your game: a comfort in times of crisis and an important factor in lowering your handicap.

▼ Before you tee off, always go through your personal pre-shot routine. It will make you feel comfortable and more confident before hitting the ball.

Keep records

When analyzing a particular round, try awarding yourself marks out of ten for each part of the game. This will help you to identify your strengths and weaknesses. You can then record this information on a chart and update it on a regular basis. Focus on raising the marks awarded for each area to a consistently high level. You should soon notice an improvement in your scoring.

▼ Some people thrive in competition and rise to the challenge while others go to pieces. Always try to stay calm and relaxed, whatever the pressure, and you will develop the ability to cope with bad shots and play to your true potential.

Target awareness

How do you react when you are studying your next shot? Do you, like the top pros, spend a lot of time looking at the target area? it will not change its shape but this will help build a strong awareness of the landing area and enable you to visualize your ball homing in on its target. This is essential to playing well as it creates a strong, positive focus for your attention. Don't just concentrate on the technicalities of how to swing your club; develop your target awareness and your ball will land much closer to the pin.

Competition

Some golfers play well against themselves but go to pieces in matches when they are unable to reproduce their normal, everyday form. Conversely, a lucky few have the ability to raise their game on such occasions and seem to reserve their best performance for when they are competing. Frequent winners, whether of the monthly medal or major championships, these golfers appear to need the stimulus of competition to inspire them.

Most people, however, tend to strike the ball better in practice than during a round, and the more competitive and pressurized that round becomes, the worse they play. The answer to their problem lies more in their state of mind than their

technique. Your mental state affects your physical actions and if you are feeling tense or anxious, then your swing may be over-tight and lacking in fluency. Fear of failure can cause you to steer the ball rather than swinging the club freely, creating inconsistent striking and, consequently, poor shots.

Create a comfort zone

Being anxious to do well in a competition may cause you to try harder than normal, transporting you out of your normal comfort zone in which you tend to perform best. If you are more confident on the practice tee, try to imagine yourself back on the practice ground and swing accordingly with the right amount of effort and concentration.

If you play better in a friendly fourball, take a few deep breaths and clear your mind of all other thoughts. Now visualize yourself about to play the same stroke but in much more comfortable circumstances. If you feel relaxed and comfortable about your game, then you will swing better and play to your true capabilities.

Analyze your game

When your round is over, don't just forget all about it over a drink in the clubhouse. Try to analyze your round and to learn from your experiences in order to improve your future game. Golf challenges your physical and mental abilities, providing you with the frustration of bad shots and the exhilaration of good ones.

Practising your swing and improving your technique will help you to become a better, more consistent golfer, but you must do this in a positive way or any improvement will be slow. Decide which area of your game needs to be improved and work on it. Look at the clubs you will use most frequently during a round – your putter, wedge and driver – and practise with these to develop familiarity and confidence.

▲ If in a competition your ball lands in a gorse bush, don't panic. Worrying about it will cause you to hit a bad shot and add unwanted strokes to your score. Instead, focus on hitting a good recovery shot and try to emulate the good shots you hit in practice.

want to know **more?**

Take it to the next level...

Go to...
- ▶ **Practice** – page 28
- ▶ **The swing** – page 35
- ▶ **Golf rules and etiquette** – page 182

Other sources
- ▶ **Your local golf professional**
  will play a round with you
- ▶ **Golf schools**
  combining instruction with a vacation
- ▶ **Golf masterclasses**
  run by top Tour and teaching pros
- ▶ **Magazines**
  for information on masterclasses
- ▶ **Publications**
  visit www.collins.co.uk for Collins golf books

swing faults

Most golfers encounter some problems in their game at one time or another but the good news is that these can all be remedied. Understanding what causes these faults can help you to avoid their consequences and learn how to cure them. Overcome the most dreaded bad shots and you will soon be hitting the ball again with confidence and precision.

The slice

This is the most common of all the swing faults to afflict golfers, especially beginners and high-handicap players. The ball will start its flight to the left of the intended target line and will subsequently curve severely to the right.

The cause

This is a weak shot which lacks power and often will fly higher than it should do. It curves to the right because the golfer strikes the ball with the club face open, thereby aiming off to the left.

The cause of this shot pattern is usually due to an incorrect grip and hand action which cause the club face to return to the ball in an open position, aiming to the right of the ball to target line. This causes the ball to finish right of your target. Most people's natural reaction to this is to start aiming even further left to compensate for it.

However, the more you allow for your slice, the more likely you are to perpetuate it. It is a vicious circle because by aiming considerably left, your swing path is likely to go the same way and you must deliver the club face in an open position, or the ball will fly straight left.

The remedy

When you set up, your left hand should hold the grip in the fingers, but not too tightly. The 'V's between the thumb and first finger of both hands should point towards your right shoulder, not your chin. Your feet and shoulders should be parallel to the target line, and your left shoulder

▶ This sequence shows the slice. The weak grip and poor alignment cause the club to go back outside the ball to target line, sending the ball to the right.

should be higher than the right one. You must not position the ball too far forward in your stance as this will contribute to an open club face; it should be further back towards the right foot.

The swing

Beware of rolling your hands and opening the club face on the takeaway; make a more rounded, flatter swing. At the top of the backswing, the club face should be on the same angle as the shoulder plane. Make sure you make a full shoulder turn, with your weight on the right leg.

On the downswing, swing the club down from the top with your hands and arms from the inside, moving your arms in unison close to the right hip. On the throughswing, move your arms away from the left hip to clear the left side. The back of the left hand and forearm should rotate within the arc of the swing, and the club shaft must point downwards on the follow through as your weight shifts onto your firm left leg.

▲ These hands are in a weak position as they are turned too far to the left. Correct your grip by moving both hands to the right so the 'V's are pointing more towards your right shoulder than your chin. Do not grip the handle too tightly.

The hook

Unlike the slice, which tends to afflict beginners and poor players, the hook is associated more with good golfers and can be devastating, especially if it causes the ball to land in hazards and trouble spots around the course.

The cause

A hooked ball begins its flight to the right of the intended target line and then curves severely to the left. It tends to fly lower and to land with topspin, making it a particularly destructive shot because it runs further off-line. All hooked shots are hit with the club face closed at impact, causing them to bend to the left when airborne.

Hooking is often associated with a strong grip: holding the club with the left hand too far on top of the grip and the right hand too far under. This results in the club face returning to the ball in a closed position (aiming left of the target), creating a swing plane that is too flat on the backswing and too upright on the follow through. Because most right-handed golfers are considerably stronger in their right hand, it tends to take over, causing the left hand and wrist to collapse.

When things go wrong in golf, our natural reaction to try and put things rights often has the opposite effect and makes them worse. In this case, most golfers aim too far right in their set up to compensate. A strong grip will cause the face of the club at the top of the backswing to be pointing skywards in a closed position. This will be reflected at impact when the bottom of the swing arc arrives too early behind the ball and, combined with the swing path going right of target, imparts anti-clockwise spin on the ball.

▶ The backswing of the hooker is too flat, causing the club face to return to the ball in a closed position, aiming left of the target, and the follow through to be too upright.

MUST KNOW

Equipment check
Make sure you check the following first:
- The lie of your club may be too upright.
- The grip may be too thin.
- The club shaft may be too flexible.
- Your ball may be too far back in your stance.

The remedy

At address, weaken your grip and position the ball forward in your stance to eliminate a flat swing plane and align your shoulders more to the left. The back of your left hand should face the target. Your right hand should be holding more in the fingers (palm facing the target) with light pressure. Grip the club with your hands turned more to the left, the 'V's pointing at your chin. Your feet, knees, hips and shoulders should aim slightly left of target.

The swing

Make your swing path straighter on the backswing. At the top, both wrists should be under the shaft with the toe of the club face pointing downwards. On the downswing, your hips and body should turn to face left of target; as you swing down you must clear the left side. Your hands should swing left of your left shoulder at the finish. Keep your left hand and wrist firm through impact, the back of your left hand facing the target. The right hand must not overtake and cross over the left too soon.

▲ The grip is too strong and the hands are turned too far to the right. The left hand is too far on top of the grip and the right hand is too far underneath it. If both 'V's point near to or outside the right shoulder, move them to the left. When you look down at your left hand, you should see two knuckles. If your grip is too strong, you may see three or even more.

The pull

A pulled shot will always fly in a straight line to the left of your intended target. The club face is square relative to the swing path, and therefore you do not impart any sidespin on the ball, causing an outside-to-in swing path.

MUST KNOW

Check your swing

● First of all, always check your set up as usual: grip, stance, aim, alignment and ball position.

● On the backswing, make sure your left shoulder, arms and club head must all start moving as one.

● At the top of your backswing, the shaft of the club should be parallel to the target line.

● Keep the club head moving inside the intended line of flight on the downswing.

▶ The swing path for the pull. The club lying on the grass behind the ball shows the correct target line. The club to the left of the ball shows the swing path of the pull with the ball finishing left of the target.

The cause

The pull is closely related to the slice as the swing path is the same, but it should not be confused with the hook just because the ball has finished left of target. A pulled hook will start out travelling to the left and then curl even further left before the ball lands. Some golfers find that they slice with their long straighter-faced clubs and pull the shorter ones. This is because the lofted clubs impart backspin which reduces the amount of sidespin which is associated with the longer clubs.

The remedy

You must concentrate on your swing path which is moving across your body on an out-to-in line. You need to stop swinging the club head across the line of the ball's intended flight. Start off by checking your aim at address: you may find that your feet, shoulders and club face are aiming to the left. Check the ball position also; it must not be too far forward in your stance and it should be positioned inside the left heel.

The swing

Your backswing should be on a more rounded, flatter plane and you must make a full shoulder turn. Your shoulders, arms, hands and club head should all move together in one piece around a fixed axis so that the club head starts moving inside the intended line of ball flight. At the top of the backswing the club shaft should be parallel to the intended target line.

On the downswing, return on the same path, with your arms close to the right hip and transfer your weight from your right side to the left. At impact, the club should have reached maximum speed and will swing towards the target. On the throughswing, the arms should move away from the left hip. Adopt a higher finishing position.

▲ To cure the pull, you need a more rounded backswing on a flatter plane and a full shoulder turn to keep the club on an inside path. On the downswing, you should return on the same path and transfer your weight to the left foot. Halfway through the downswing, if you have reached the right position, then you have no choice but to hit the ball from the inside.

The push

This usually occurs when you move your body ahead of the ball before impact, causing the ball to fly in a straight line to the right of the target. This should not to be confused with a slice although the ball finishes in a similar place.

The cause

This belongs to the same family as the hook but the club face is square relative to the swing path instead of being closed. If you do this, you are not imparting any spin on the ball which simply flies straight in the direction of your swing path.

The push is usually due to one of two faults: swaying to the left on the downswing, causing your body and hands to be in front of the club head when it hits the ball, or positioning the ball too far back in your stance towards the right foot.

The remedy

Check your set up: your feet, shoulders and club face may be aiming to the right. Check the ball is not too far back in your stance or too far right of centre. Check that your grip is not too weak with either or both hands too far round to the left which will cause the club face to open through the shot.

The swing

On the backswing, make your swing path straighter to achieve a more upright position. Do not sway; swing the club head on an inclined plane, starting on an inside path close to the grass with the club face facing the ball for a more upright backswing and more effective downswing. The follow through should be more rounded with the hips turned and your stomach facing the target or slightly to the left of it. Do not arch your back too much on the follow through. Your hands should swing to the left of your left shoulder at the finish.

▲ The swing path for the push. The club on the grass behind the ball indicates the correct target line. The club to the left of the ball shows the swing path of the push with the ball finishing right of your intended target. The push shot does not curve in flight; it starts to the right of your target and continues to the right. If your set up is good and you still hit a push shot, check your swing. It may be you are swinging on an in-to-out path with the club face square to that line.

Topping

This relatively common swing fault is experienced by some beginners who often hit the ball straight along the ground. You may well be afflicted by this shot if you attempt to lift the ball in a scooping action to help get it airborne.

The cause

This occurs when the ball is struck above its equator by an ascending club head, producing a very low shot. Loft is built into a golf club head and you do not need to compensate for lack of loft and have to 'lift' the ball into the air yourself.

The remedy

For iron shots, especially mid to short irons (5–pw), strike the ball on the downswing with the club head descending, taking a divot after the ball. Touch the turf at least with the sole of the club to contact the ball squarely in the middle of the club face.

The swing

Your backswing should be more upright. Check it has not become too flat with you swinging your arms around your body on too rounded an arc. To swing downwards on to the ball, the club head must swing on a straighter line back and up on the backswing. Pull down with the left arm to start the downswing and ensure the wrists uncock fully so the club head gets back to the bottom of the ball. Transfer your weight from your right side to the left on the downswing to strike the ball on a downward path. Your hands should be ahead of the club head at impact.

Practise striking balls with a 3 wood or 6 iron, focusing on making contact with the club head behind the bottom of the ball. At or just before impact, your left arm and the club shaft should be in a straight line.

▲ Topping occurs when the ball is struck above its equator, causing it to travel along the ground. Instead of the ball being struck on the downswing with the club head descending and taking a divot after the ball, in a topped shot it is hit on the upswing by an ascending club head; no divot is taken.

Skying

This shot is not really common and it happens only when the ball is teed up using a driver. The flight is extremely high but with little forward momentum, the ball soaring up impressively into the sky but not travelling very far.

▲ The moment of impact for a normal swing as opposed to a skied shot (opposite).

The cause

A skied shot is caused by striking the ball with the top part of the club face, often scratching the head. Most of us, at some time in our golfing lives, have tried to hit the ball further than is humanly possible, leading to a steep backswing and a subsequent chop down into the ball.

If the club approaches the ball from too steep an angle on the downswing and the front edge of the sole of the club hits into the ground, the result will be a skied shot. When hitting wood shots, the club should be swept away without hitting the ground unlike iron shots which should be struck on the downswing with a divot after the ball. The shaft of a wood is longer than that of an iron and will produce a bigger circle with a wider arc for the club head. Thus the sole of the club head can be parallel to the ground at the bottom of the swing arc. If you position the ball forward in your stance – opposite your left instep for a driver – your contact will be at the correct angle to sweep the ball forwards instead of chopping down and producing a skied shot.

The remedy

At address, make sure that you position the ball forward in your stance. Some people worry about the height of the tee and believe that teeing the ball high will produce a skied shot but this is not necessarily the case. The important thing is to keep the club head travelling parallel to the ground for several inches before impact. The loft

◄ The moment of impact for a skied shot which occurs when the downswing is very steep and too much club face is below the centre of the ball at impact. Instead of sweeping the ball away on an in-to-out path, the club chops down on the ball from too steep an angle. Swinging smoothly, keeping the club head low to the ground at the start of the backswing and parallel to the ground just before impact, can prevent this.

of the club face will lift the ball up into the air; it does not need any help from you. At set up, keep your hands level with the back of the ball with the sole of your club resting flat on the ground.

The swing

At the start of the backswing, keep the club head low to the ground, and do not break the wrists too early. Make your backswing plane flatter than usual; it should be a more rounded shallow arc. Transfer your weight onto the right side at the top of the backswing and keep your head behind the ball until after impact. Don't try to scoop the ball up which will produce contact below the centre of the ball; you need a low sweep with a slight curve at the beginning of the backswing.

▶ # Toeing

This swing fault can affect all golfers at some time or another and you will know immediately when it happens because you will feel the club shaft twisting in your hands at impact.

The cause

Toeing occurs when the toe end of the club strikes the inside half of the ball, causing a shot that flies straight to the right with little power, even though the club face may well be square. A toed shot may appear to be similar to a shank.

Get your balance right

To produce this shot, the club head will have been swung on an out-to-in swing path, causing it to return to a point closer to you than at address. This is sometimes caused by incorrect balance in the set up. If you stand too close to the ball it will result too much of your weight being on your heels at address and as you return the ball. Conversely, if you stand too far away from the ball, it will make it impossible for your arms to reach the ball. Try to analyze which of these two scenarios applies to you: whether your weight is mainly on your heels or your toes.

▲ Standing too close to the ball can cause toeing. Too much weight is on your heels at address. Standing the correct distance from the ball makes you swing on a slightly inclined plane, causing the club head to move on an in-to-out swing path. Move your feet a little at address to settle them into the correct position.

Ideally, your weight should be distributed evenly between your heels and the balls of your feet, and this is influenced by the distance you stand from the ball. So don't stand in the same way for every shot as this will lead to many poor and erratic hits which are way off target.

Get settled

When addressing the ball, move your feet to get settled. Do not plant them down in a really solid position and stand motionless before you swing. Have a few waggles with the club head and shuffle your feet slightly to fine tune your balance.

Practice drill

A helpful drill for correcting toeing is to substitute two tees for the ball, one of which should be about a ball's width further from you than the other. Address the closer tee towards the toe of the club and make a swing that returns to strike both tees. This will encourage contact with the centre of the club face.

The remedy

When you set up, check your balance and distance from the ball. You should not stand too far from it at address as this can result in an out-to-in swing path on a flat plane. You will lose power as you reach out to try and make contact.

The swing

You want to swing slightly under yourself on an inclined plane. If your grip, stance and ball position are correct, start making your backswing. The club head should stay close to the ground on a slight curve for about 25 cm (10 in). At the top of the backswing your left shoulder should have turned 90 degrees to arrive under your chin.

Swing back down to the ball and through, keeping the left arm extended through impact and maintaining your spine angle. Swing your arms freely away from your body.

▲ Practise this simple drill with two tees instead of a ball. Address the closer tee towards the toe of the club and then swing smoothly so the club face strikes both tees centrally at impact.

MUST KNOW

Toeing checklist
- At set up, always check your stance and grip.
- Check that the ball position is correct for the club you are using.
- Check that you are standing the right distance from the ball; not too far away nor too close.
- Think of making a circle as you swing back from the ball at address.
- Check that your left shoulder is under your chin at the top of the backswing.
- Swing the club head smoothly down inside the intended line of flight.
- Don't scoop the ball into the air. Drive down through it.

Hitting behind the ball

This fault, which is also referred to as 'hitting fat, is often experienced by golfers. The club head hits the ground behind the ball and the cushion of turf between the club face and ball leads to a severe loss of distance.

▲ Hitting behind the ball can be caused by falling back onto the heels and trying to lift the ball while dipping. Avoid by keeping your left side firm at the bottom of your swing. Keep the left leg straight to support your weight as you rotate towards the target. Do not scoop the ball but keep your left forearm, wrist and back of hand in line.

The cause

This fault can be caused by falling back onto your heels and trying to lift the ball into the air at impact. To prevent this, keep your left side firm at the bottom of your swing. Do not try to 'get under the ball' – allow the loft of the club face to lift it. Visualize your swing arc as a 'U' shape on a slant with the bottom of the 'U' coming after the ball. It is possible that you hit behind the ball because your backswing is too upright and flat. If your divot is very deep and behind the ball, this may well be the case and your backswing is creating a steep angle of attack into the ball.

Practice drill

Try placing a second golf ball approximately 30 cm (12 in) behind your ball to encourage a downward strike. If you bottom out behind the correct ball, you will contact the wrong one.

The remedy

When you set up for your swing, make your usual checks at address. Swing back smoothly, gripping the club with the same pressure in both hands. This will help prevent separation between the hands at the top of the backswing which may lead to a 'casting' action on the downswing. Pull down and through towards the target with your left arm, maintaining the left forearm, wrist and back of hand in line through impact. Keep your left leg straight supporting your weight, while your hips rotate to face the target.

MUST KNOW

The golden rule
A useful rule to bear in mind is: if the divot is deep, swing flatter. If the divot is shallow, swing more upright.

The overswing

This happens when you swing the club back too far and it travels beyond the horizontal at the top of the backswing so you are in a position where you lose control. This causes loss of length and power and striking the ground behind the ball.

The cause

A common cause is excessive wrist break and letting go of the club or opening up with your left hand at the top of your backswing. To avoid this, keep your takeaway slow and smooth to get into the correct position. Do not lose control by swinging the club back too quickly. In an effort to stop overswinging, you may fail to turn your shoulders and body fully, which will lead to yet more problems and varied, inconsistent shots.

Practice drill

If you have a tendency to overswing, you should try hitting a few balls with a 6 or 7 iron, focusing on keeping your hands and wrists active from the moment you start moving the club back at address. Make sure you break your wrists early in the takeaway to set yourself up for a more controlled and powerful downswing.

The remedy

Set up for your shot with the left-hand grip held firmly in the base of the fingers (excluding the index finger). Concentrate on using your hands and wrists earlier in the downswing.

The swing

Swing back slowly, keeping the club head close to the ground in the first part of the takeaway. Your takeaway should not be too steep; keep the club head moving on a shallow arc and break the wrists early for a more powerful downswing.

▲ The club shaft has gone below the horizontal position. The left arm has bent too much during the backswing and the swing is now out of control. You should keep your left arm as straight as possible. Overswinging may also be caused by excessive wrist break.

The shank

The most destructive and dreaded shot of all, the shank has shattered the confidence of many golfers. However, it is relatively easy to cure and, although it is nerve-wracking, you can take comfort in the fact that most good players have experienced it at some time in their lives.

▲ Shanking may be caused by returning to the ball with the club face very closed (top), or by returning with the club face very open (above). Both cause the hosel to strike the ball rather than the club face.

The cause

It occurs when the ball is struck from the socket of the club head where the face meets the hosel, causing it to career to the right at a severe angle, usually low. The shank is a difficult fault to analyze as there are three possible causes:

● Returning to the ball with the club face very open.
● Returning to the ball with the club face very closed.
● Returning with the club head to the ball further from you than at address.

Whichever of these faults applies to you, you will probably find that your weight is moving onto your toes with your knees bent. To avoid this, you should keep your weight towards your heels during the downswing and follow through.

Identifying your fault

If the club face returns in a very open position, the heel and hosel will arrive at the ball first. If the club face is very closed, it will approach on too rounded an arc and can gather the ball into the socket of the club. Consider which ball flight you tend to produce normally. If you have a tendency to slice, your shank shot will be of the open face variety; if you tend to hook, it will be the closed face version.

An occasional shank that afflicts a normally straight hitter is likely to be caused by the club head returning further away from you. The divot would still be straight and the club face square.

The remedy

The best remedy is to practise the two tees exercise for toeing (see page 165). Place two tees approximately a ball's width apart, one further away from you. Address the furthest one and make a swing that returns to strike only the tee closest to you. Practising on a slope with the ball below your feet may also be helpful if your swing tends to be too flat.

▲ The two tees exercise to cure the shank. Address the tee that is further away from you (top), then swing and strike the tee closer to you (above). Practise regularly and it will help cure this most destructive shot.

▲ The correct position for the club face and ball at address (top); and the position at impact for the shank (above) when the club face returns to the ball and strikes it on the hosel, causing it to fly low and to the right.

Easy-to-make faults

To improve your golf, you need not only to analyze what causes your bad shots so that you can remedy the problem but also to look at simple causes such as how you address the ball: your body alignment and posture. Practise them on the practice ground before venturing out on to the course.

Body alignment

Many golfers persist in believing that their feet and body should aim at the target. However, it is the club face that should be aimed at the target; the feet, knees, hips and shoulders should be parallel to the club face-to-target line.

Posture

Good posture can help you to control your swing plane by promoting balance and the correct weight distribution. Keep your head steady, but not down, and remember to keep your chin up, your back straight, and bend from your hips.

Posture check

Stand erect and hold the club shaft near the head of the club with your right hand. Place the club shaft against your back from the base of your spine to the back of your head and then bend forwards from your hips. Keep the back of your head touching the shaft for as long as possible and only allow it to leave the line sufficiently to look down to see the ball. Flex your knees slightly and your arms should be able to hang downwards from your shoulders, clear of your body.

◀ Don't set up with your legs too straight (top) nor stoop over the ball (centre). Your knees should be slightly flexed and the weight evenly distributed between both feet (bottom). Don't have your hands too low nor too high; your arms must be able to swing the club freely and clear of your body. Your legs should not feel too stiff nor too straight.

◀ In the reverse pivot, the body weight will shift to the left rather than the right side during the backswing.

Reverse pivot

Pivoting your body correctly on the backswing will transfer most of your weight onto your right leg. The pivot point is the right hip. However, you should always try to avoid making the mistake of straightening your right leg and bending your left knee forwards towards a point in front of the ball as this will cause too much weight to stay on your left leg at the top of the backswing. If you want to give your swing power and club head speed, then your weight should travel in the direction of the swing.

Obviously, you cannot transfer your weight from the right side to the left if it is already on your left leg on the backswing, and the result will be that you will end up toppling backwards with a lot of weight on your right foot and you will lose forward momentum and power. To prevent this happening, check carefully that your posture, weight distribution and backswing are correct. Refer back to the chapter on the swing.

want to know more?

Take it to the next level...

Go to...
▶ **The set up** – page 36
▶ **The swing** – page 45
▶ **Body action** – page 46

Other sources
▶ **Your local golf professional**
  for eradicating swing faults
▶ **Driving ranges**
  for practising your swing
▶ **Golf masterclasses**
  for perfecting your swing
▶ **Internet**
  for interactive swing CD-ROMs
▶ **Publications**
  visit www.collins.co.uk for Collins golf books

golf rules

& etiquette

We can all benefit from a better understanding of the Rules of golf and how they are applied. As well as increasing your enjoyment of the game, it can save you strokes and lower your scores. This section will give you a basic appreciation of the most commonly used Rules to help you deal with a range of different situations that you will encounter out on the golf course.

Etiquette

**Good golfers show consideration towards their fellow players.
They treat them with respect, are mindful of their safety
and take good care of the course. How you behave is very
important. Always treat others as you would wish to be
treated and leave the course as you would wish to find it.**

Replacing divots

If you are hitting a shot from the tee or fairway you will often take a divot.
This is a piece of turf that is dislodged when your club strikes the ground
behind the ball. On the fairway, divots must be replaced quickly and
trodden down firmly so the turf can take root and grow again. If it is left,
after 24 hours the grass will die and the course will be scarred. However,
you need not replace a divot on the tee.

Pitch marks

If you play a high approach shot to the green, the impact of the ball may
leave an indentation on the putting surface, which is known as a pitch
mark. It is good golf etiquette to repair this immediately with a pitch mark
repairer – carry one in your pocket or golf bag. Just lever the grass around
the indentation back into position, then flatten it with the sole of your
putter. You can use a tee peg for this if you don't have a repairer.

Be considerate

You should always treat your companions with
consideration. Don't stand too close when they
are taking a practice swing, and stand quietly to
the side when they are playing their shots – do
not speak or start playing with the coins in your
pocket. If you watch the flight of their ball, you
can help search for it if it gets lost.

There may be a group behind you waiting to
play; don't hold them up by standing around
working out your scores after taking your shots.
Move off briskly and do this en route to the next
tee. Similarly, don't hit your shot while the group
in front is still in range. If you use a trolley, park it
to the side; don't take it on to the tee or green.

MUST KNOW

Raking bunkers
When you leave a
bunker, always rake
the sand thoroughly
to leave it smooth. If
there is no rake, use
your shoe or the sole
of your golf club.
Any players coming
up behind you
should not see any
signs that you have
been there.

On the tee

The coloured markers on the teeing ground indicate where you should play from. Men usually play off the yellow tees while women play off the red and seniors and juniors off the blue ones. White tees are for medal or other competitions. You can tee up your ball anywhere within a rectangle two club lengths back from the markers. You may stand outside the teeing ground to play a ball within it.

Taking a stroke

If you swing the club with the express intention of hitting the ball, the stroke will count, but if you take a practice swing and hit the ground with your club in such a way that the ball falls off the tee, you will not take a penalty. This is because you were not attempting to hit he ball.

If the ball falls off the tee before you take a stroke, then you will not be penalized because the ball is not in play. However, if it falls off the tee while your club head is descending and you miss it completely, the stroke will count but you will not have to add a penalty.

While you are on the tee, it is a good idea to make a mental note of which ball you are using by checking its make and number. This will make it easier to identify if it gets lost or lands in a clump of other balls. And remember that golf etiquette decrees that whoever scores best on the previous hole has 'the honour' of teeing off first on the next one.

▲ When teeing off, you can place the ball anywhere within a rectangle two club lengths back from the markers.

Off the tee

When you move away from the tee out on to the course, different rules apply if you address the ball and it moves. Even if you are taking a practice swing or have stood over the ball as if to hit it and have grounded your club, you will be penalized one stroke. To prevent this happening, never rest your club on the ground behind the ball.

Out of bounds

If you tee up your ball and it goes out of bounds (OB), you add a penalty stroke to your score for losing the ball and you must tee up another. If, at any time on the course, you hit a ball OB or lose it, you do exactly the same – add a penalty stroke and play your next shot from where you played the previous one, known as 'stroke and distance'.

Provisional ball

If you hit a shot that disappears from sight, you can assume that it might be lost and are permitted to hit another ball – a provisional ball. If you cannot find the original ball, you may continue play with the provisional one. If this happens to you, just wait until your companions have played their shots and then tell them that you plan to play a 'provisional ball' - you must use those words and make it clear what you are intending to do. If your first shot travelled, say, 200 yards before going out of sight and the provisional goes only

MUST KNOW

Defining OB
This refers to an area into which you are not allowed to venture and from which play is prohibited. It is defined by white stakes or a line on the ground. If a ball lands OB it is unplayable. However, you may stand out of bounds in order to play a ball that is in bounds.

MUST KNOW

OB boundaries
● Usually OB markers define the boundaries of a golf course but sometimes areas within the course, such as a practice fairway between two holes, can be defined as OB.
● The score card you collect from the pro shop has local rules printed on the back. Check these before you play to find out where the OB boundaries are.

100 yards, you can hit the provisional as often as necessary until it reaches, or goes beyond, the spot where the original is likely to be.

Lost ball

If your ball is lost in the general course of play, you are allowed five minutes in which to look for it. However, if it is lost, you must play 'stroke and distance', i.e. add another stroke to your score and hit the next shot from the same place where you played the last one. If you fail to find a lost ball in a clump of trees or the rough, you are not allowed to drop another ball on the edge of the fairway and take a penalty stroke.

Many golfers choose to ignore this Rule because they do not wish to trudge all the way back to the place from which they played their original shot. However, you don't have to do this because you can play with a provisional ball (see opposite), which will now become the ball in play. When you add up your score for the hole, count the number of strokes you play with the provisional ball plus the number taken with the original ball, and a penalty stroke.

▼ The white lines on the ground denote the area that is out of bounds and within which play is prohibited. it may also be defined by some white stakes.

GOLF RULES & ETIQUETTE

177

Slow play

One of the most common causes of slow play is not calling through the next group if you get delayed searching for a lost ball. As soon as you realize that your original ball is lost, you should wave through the following match. Do this by waving your arm to catch their attention. You must let them play past you, even if you find your ball just after waving them through.

Definitions of a lost ball

Declaring that your ball is lost is meaningless unless you fulfil one of the conditions below. A ball can only become lost if:

● You cannot find it within five minutes.

● You make a stroke at a provisional ball beyond the point where the original is likely to be.

● You put another ball into play, e.g. not clearly declaring that you are playing a provisional.

Searching for a ball

The Rules allow five minutes to search for your ball but sometimes it may be moved in the process of looking for it. This may happen if you, your playing partner or either of your caddies touch or bend the long grass or heather where the ball is nestling; if so, you will incur a penalty stroke and must replace the ball. However, if the ball is moved by your opponent (in matchplay) or anyone on his/her team or by a fellow competitor in strokeplay you do not incur a penalty. In either case the ball must be replaced.

Obstructions

In golf, an obstruction is defined as anything artificial such as benches, the side of roads and paths, cigarette ends and tin cans. The only exceptions to this are objects that define out of bounds, any part of an immovable man-made object that is out of bounds, and any construction declared to be an integral part of the course. If you are not sure, then you should look at the local rules on the back of your scorecard.

You may take relief from an obstruction anywhere on the course with the exception of immovable obstructions in water hazards. If the obstruction is movable, you are permitted to move it without being penalized. If the ball is moved in

▼ If you find that your ball has landed in an unplayable position, such as in a gorse bush, you should declare it unplayable to your playing partners. Measure two club lengths away from the spot where it has landed – but no nearer the hole – and then, holding your ball at shoulder height, drop it on to the ground. Now take your shot but remember that you will incur a one-stroke penalty and you must add this to your score.

Obstructions
These are artificial, man-made objects. If an immovable object interferes with your stance or intended swing path on the course, you make take relief without penalty within one club length. If the obstruction is movable you may dispose of it without penalty. In contrast, a loose impediment is a natural object that can be moved at any time outside a hazard as long as you do not move the ball as well.

▼ Leaves, twigs and long
grass are natural objects,
and you can remove these
loose impediments at any
time unless they are in a
hazard (a bunker or water
hazard). Note that if they are
within a club length of your
ball and the ball moves, you
will be penalized one stroke.

the process of moving the object, you may
replace it. If your ball was on or in the obstruction,
after removing the obstruction, you must drop the
ball as near as possible to the spot where it lay –
the exception to this rule is on the green where
you place rather than drop it. However, if the
obstruction is not movable, as in the case of a
telegraph pole or a pylon, and it interferes with
your stance or your intended line of swing, you are
allowed to take relief without incurring a penalty.

Taking relief

First, find the nearest point of relief, which is not
nearer the hole, avoids any interference or
requiring you to drop in a hazard or on a putting
green, and drop your ball within one club length
of that point. Hopefully, you should end up taking
the same kind of shot as you would if the
obstruction had not been there.

If you drop the ball twice and are still not able
to take your shot as is the case when a ball
keeps rolling into a bunker, you may place the
ball on the spot where it landed the second time
you dropped it.

Luckily for you, the Rules do not distinguish
between the fairway, rough, trees and other
parts of the course, so if your ball is nestling up
against a telegraph pole in some deep rough

◄ The sprinkler head does not interfere with the player's stance or intended line of swing (left) and therefore there is no relief. He may take relief (right) because his stance would be on the sprinkler head.

◄ Find the nearest point of relief and measure out one club length in order to drop from the ground under relief.

and your nearest point of relief is on the fairway, think yourself fortunate. The golden rule to remember is that 'nearest point of relief' refers to relief from the obstruction; however, if that happens to be in the middle of a large patch of wiry heather or a gorse bush, you have to accept it and play accordingly.

Dropping the ball

You should stand with your arm straight out at shoulder height and drop it within one club length of the nearest point of relief. It may roll up to a further two club lengths away, as long as it goes no nearer the hole. The only exceptions to this are dropping in an unplayable lie or from a lateral water hazard, in which case you may drop within two club lengths and the ball may roll up to two club lengths away but no nearer the hole.

▲ When taking a drop, you must stand upright with the ball held at shoulder height.

Competition

There are specific Rules that relate to competition, notably matchplay and strokeplay. The former is usually more popular and involves two players or two teams playing hole by hole.

Matchplay and strokeplay

In matchplay, if you have the higher handicap and play the first hole in four strokes whereas your opponent takes five, you will win the hole and are one up. You continue playing until one player or team is more holes ahead than there are left to play. In strokeplay, however, every golfer plays against the course and keeps track of their strokes during a round. The Rules legislate for both and the penalty for infringements differs. In matchplay the most common penalty is loss of hole; in strokeplay, it is two penalty strokes.

Handicap

This enables players of different abilities can compete on equal terms on the same course. Thus if your average score over a par 72 course is 92, your handicap would be 20 (92 minus 72). If you played against someone with a 2 handicap, shooting 74 (par plus 2), and you played one under your handicap, scoring a total of 91, you would win, despite taking a higher overall score. In matchplay, he would 'give' you 18 strokes (the difference between your handicaps), so you would receive a stroke a hole, i.e. if he takes four on the first hole and you take five, the hole is halved. If you both take four, you win. This assumes you are playing off full handicap, but in matchplay in England you are often only given three-quarters of the difference of handicap; in strokeplay, seven-eighths.

Number of clubs

You are only allowed to carry a maximum of 14 clubs in your bag. If you start with less, you may add extra clubs until you reach that number. If you break a club accidentally, you may replace it so long as you do not delay play unduly. However, it must be an accident; if you miss a shot and slam your club into the ground in anger, snapping off the head, you cannot replace it.

If you are found to have more than 14 clubs, you are penalized two strokes for each hole you play with the wrong number but there is a maximum four-stroke penalty in any round. However, if you realize that you have an extra club at the beginning of the round, declare this and do not use it during the round, that is permissible.

Hazards

We all want to get the ball from tee to green and into the hole in as few strokes as possible, hopefully by avoiding any bunkers or water hazards that lie in wait to trap the unwary. Many of the Rules relating to hazards are different from those that apply elsewhere on the golf course.

Bunkers

You cannot ground your club in a hazard so when you are in a bunker or any kind of water hazard, make sure you keep your club above the surface of the ground when taking up your stance. Even brushing the sand in a bunker as you take your club head back will incur two penalty strokes.

A grass island within a bunker is not part of the bunker. You may therefore ground your club while addressing the ball if it is sitting on the grass. From casual water in a bunker, the maximum available relief is permitted, not complete relief.

Water hazards

These may be ordinary or lateral. Whereas ordinary water hazards are marked by yellow stakes or lines, lateral ones are indicated by red stakes or lines. Water hazards are at some point between you and the green, whereas lateral hazards run laterally to, or in the same direction as, the hole.

▲ When addressing the ball in a bunker, be careful not to ground your club (top). If your club brushes the sand (above) as you take it back, then you will be penalized two strokes.

Lost ball in a water hazard

If you lose a ball in a water hazard (yellow stakes or lines), remember the following easy formula: 'Play, replay or as far back as you like'.

- **Play** means you can play the ball as it lies, so if the ball is lying on a grass bank leading down to the water, this might be a realistic option.
- **Replay** means 'stroke and distance', i.e. go back to where you played your last shot and play it again, adding a penalty stroke to your score.
- **As far back as you like'** means that if your ball is in, touching or lost in a water hazard, you must make a mental note of the point where it crossed the boundary of the water hazard and may then drop the ball or

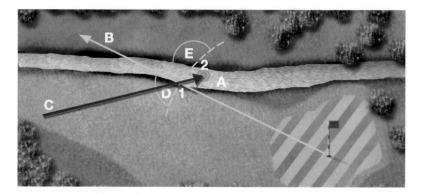

▲ For a lateral water hazard your options are: take the point where the ball last crossed the margin of the hazard (1) and drop the ball within two club lengths of that point, no nearer the hole. Or you may drop it on the opposite margin of the hazard, equidistant from the hole (2). The hazard is A; B is a line backwards from the point where the ball last crossed the margin of the hazard; C is the ball flight path from the tee; D and E are additional dropping areas.

MUST KNOW

Taking a drop
If you drop on the far side of a lateral water hazard, it must be opposite the point where the ball crossed the hazard, but the same distance from the hole as that point.

another ball (if it is lost) on a line that keeps the point where it last crossed the margin of the hazard between you and the hole, going as far back as you wish in a straight line. You also add a penalty stroke to your score. Do not retrace the ball's flight; just stand at the spot where your ball last crossed the boundary of the hazard, then turn towards the hole and walk backwards as far as you want before dropping another ball.

Lateral water hazards

A lateral water hazard runs laterally to, or in the same direction as, the hole. The stakes or lines defining the hazard are in the hazard. The 'As far back as you like' option may not be possible if your ball ends up in a this hazard because it may mean you walking backwards down the hazard. If so, you will have the three options ('Play, replay and as far back as you like'), plus two more.

You can mark the spot mentally where the ball crossed the boundary of the hazard and can measure up to two club lengths away – with your longest club to get maximum advantage – and drop within that distance. When the ball hits the ground it can roll up to a further two club lengths away but cannot roll nearer the hole.

Or you can drop on the far side of the hazard, within two club lengths.Whichever you choose to do, you add a penalty stroke to your score.

GOLF RULES & ETIQUETTE

The putting green

There are some specific Rules that you may need to know when your ball finally lands on the putting green. What applies on the green is often very different to anywhere else on the course but you should be aware of the following.

General Rules

You should not touch the line of your putt, i.e. the line along which you intend your ball to travel on its way to the hole. The exceptions to this Rule are: lifting your ball or pressing down a ball marker, measuring to see who is furthest from the hole, moving or brushing aside sand, loose impediments or any movable obstructions, and repairing pitch marks. You may touch the ground in front of the ball with your putter head when addressing the ball.

At any time on the putting surface you may mark your ball by placing a marker or coin behind it. You can then lift the ball and, if necessary, clean it.

If you are putting from on the green and the ball hits the flagstick, you will be penalized two strokes so ask someone to tend it for you. They should stand still with their feet away from the hole and remove the flag as your ball approaches. If you are putting or playing off the green, you may leave the flagstick in the hole if wished and will not be penalized if your ball strikes it.

Removing loose impediments

Loose impediments are natural objects, such as leaves, twigs and stones, and you are permitted to remove these from your intended line. Sand is a loose impediment on the green but nowhere else on the course. On long putts, remove any debris that will clearly affect a rolling ball although only to an extent that is practicable. On short putts of six to eight feet which you expect to hole, remove as many loose impediments as possible if time allows.

While you remove loose impediments from your line, be careful not to transfer them on to your partner's line. For putts with considerable break,

◀ You may remove any loose impediments, man-made or natural, that are on your intended line of putt from the green at any time.

you must visualize the line the ball will take so you can remove any debris from its path. If you take a practice stroke and wet grass or leaves become stuck to the putter face, either wipe the face with your finger or brush it across your trouser leg – a ball struck with debris on the putter face will often stop halfway to the hole.

On the green, loose impediments can be swept away with your hand or the putter head but not with a towel, hat or anything else. Remember, that you cannot move a loose impediment in a hazard (bunker or water hazard). Anywhere else on the course you can move loose impediments at any time, but if they are within a club length of your ball and the ball moves, you are considered to be responsible and are penalized one stroke.

Casual water

This is any temporary accumulation of water that is visible before or after you take your stance and is not in a water hazard. It may include an overflow from a water hazard or even snow and ice. If your ball comes to rest in a good lie on the fringe of the green yet there is casual water on the green between the ball and the hole, you are not permitted to take relief as the ball does not lie in or touch the casual water, nor interfere with your stance or the area of your intended swing. If you don't want to take a drop under a one-stroke penalty, you will have to chip over the water with a lofted club.

◀ If your ball is in the line of your partner or opponent, place a marking disc behind it and remove it. Place the toe of your putter behind the marker and another marker at the heel. Remove the forward marker.

GOLF RULES & ETIQUETTE

However, if your ball comes to rest in casual water on the putting surface, you may obtain relief. Mark the spot with a tee peg and pace the distance between that spot and the hole. You can replace your ball at a point nearest to where it lay, but not nearer the hole, to give you maximum relief.

Pitch marks

Always replace your ball, never drop it, on a putting surface as taking a drop may cause a pitch mark. If you replace it, you must mark it before lifting it. Use a special pitch mark repairing tool to remove pitch marks. Insert it around the perimeter of the pitch mark and gently raise, lifting inwards. Tap down with a putter – do not use your feet as the spikes in your shoes will make indentations and it is not permitted to erase spike marks on the green.

Marking the ball

You should mark your ball when it is in the line of another player. Place a marking disc directly behind the ball and then remove your ball. Now place the toe of your putter behind the marker, and place another marker at the heel of the putter. Remove the forward marker so that the line for your partner is clear. Put your ball one, two or three club lengths back again when you re-spot it. If it lodges against a loose impediment on the green, place a marker directly behind it, then lift it and remove the impediment before replacing the ball in front of the marker.

▲ You can erase a pitch mark with a pitch mark repairer or even just a golf tee. First insert the repair tool around the perimeter of the pitch mark and, lifting inwards, raise it gently. Then tap it down with your putter until flat – don't use your golf shoe as it will leave spike marks on the green.

want to know more?

Take it to the next level...

Go to...
▶ **Overcoming hazards** – page 64
▶ **Perfect putting** – page 96
▶ **Playing a round** – page 132

Other sources
▶ **Royal and Ancient Golf Club of St Andrews, Scotland**
for a copy of the Rules of Golf
▶ **Videos and DVDs**
examine the Rules in interactive form on www.randa.org
▶ **Your local professional**
for explaining specific Rules
▶ **Magazines**
for features on the Rules
▶ **Publications**
visit www.collins.co.uk for Collins golf books

Glossary of terms

Above ground: A ball is above ground when it is not settled down in the rough, in a bunker or other hazard.

Albatross: This is a score of three under par on one hole.

Alignment: The relationship between the line to the target and the golfer's body.

Approach: A shot that is played to the green.

Apron: The grass surrounding the green that is not as short as the green but is shorter than the fairway.

At rest: When the ball has stopped moving.

Backspin: To import a backward spinning rotation to the ball to make it fly high and grip the turf when it strikes the ground to minimize bounce.

Bunker: A shallow or deep impression usually filled with sand, although it may be filled with grass or earth.

Carry: The distance to where the ball lands from which it is played.

Chip: A short, low running approach shot to the green..

Choke down: To take your grip lower on the club to get more control or less length.

Cocking the wrists: The bend or break in the wrists on the backswing.

Divot: when playing a shot, this is the piece of turf which is dug out by the club.

Dog-leg: The name for a hole which bends sharply to the right or left.

Downhill lie: When the ball is hit from a downslope.

Eagle: This is a score of two under par on one hole.

Fade: A shot that is hit from left to right.

Fat: When the club head of an iron hits the turf before the ball preventing it reaching its target.

Ground under repair: A part of the course that is marked as being unfit for play.

Hook: A shot that causes the ball to curve to the player's left.

Lie: The relationship between the position of the ball and the ground underneath it.

Loose impediments: These are natural objects, such as stones, leaves, branches and worms, which can be removed except in a hazard (bunker or water).

Mishit: A shot that is not hit exactly in the centre of the club face.

Obstructions: Any man-made or artificial object on the golf course.

Out-of-bounds: A ball that falls outside the boundaries of the course, or where play is prohibited.

Par: The estimated standard score for a hole, which is usually based on its length.

Penalty stroke: A stroke or strokes that are added to a player's score when he commits a breach of the Rules.

Pitch: A high shot played from around the green, possibly over a bunker, to the hole.

Pitch and run: This is lower than a pitch shot and, on landing short of the green, runs on towards the hole.

Pitch mark: The dent or the indentation that is caused by a ball landing on the green. Pitch marks should always be repaired.

Plugged ball: A ball resting in a depression in a bunker or the rough made on landing.

Pull: A shot that flies to the left of target.

Push: A shot that flies to the right of target.

Rough: Any grass that has been permitted to grow in order to penalize shots that are hit off-line.

Scratch: A golfer with a handicap of zero.

Semi-rough: The grass growing between the uncut rough and the fairway.

Shank: When the ball is hit with an iron at the spot where the shaft joins the club head, creating a shot played at right angles.

Sidespin: This may be right-to-left or left-to-right rotation of the ball to create a shot that bends to the left or right.

Sky: A shot when the ball is struck by a wood on the fop edge of the club causing it to fly upwards.

Slice: A ball that is hit in such a way that it flies in a curve to the right of target.

Stance: The way a player places their feet before playing a shot.

Sweet spot: A point, usually in the centre of the club face which, when it hits the ball, will make it travel further than if hit elsewhere.

Topspin: The spin caused by a ball being struck above the centre.

Trajectory: The flight of the golf ball.

Waggle: The movement of the club backwards and forwards before playing a shot.

Water hazard: A ditch, stream, river, pond, lake or the sea or anything which is deemed to be a water hazard.

Need to know more?

There is a wealth of further information available for golfers, particularly if you have access to the internet. Listed below are just some of the organizations or resources that you might find useful to help you to improve your golf.

Governing Organizations
The Royal and Ancient Golf Club of St Andrews, Fife, Scotland, KY16 9JD; tel: 01334 460000, fax: 01334 460001
www.randa.org
The governing body for the rules of the game.
Professional Golfers' Association (UK), Centenary House, The De Vere Belfry, Sutton Coldfield, West Midlands, B76 9PT; tel: 01675 470333
fax: 01675 477888
www.pga.org.uk
Professional Golfers' Association (USA)
www.pga.com
Gives details of news, tournaments, merchandise, shows, events and PGA golf schools.
PGA European Tour
www.europeantour.com
Information, statistics and news about the European Tour.

Golf Magazines
Golf Digest
The Golf Digest Companies, 20 Westport Road, PO Box 850, Wilton, Connecticut 06897, USA; tel: 203 761 5100
www.golfdigest.com
The major American golf magazine which runs its own golf schools.
Golf World, Today's Golfer, Golf Monthly, Golf Weekly, Women and Golf Magazine
Bushfield House, Orton Centre, Peterborough, PE2 5UW;
tel: 01733 237111
www.emap.com

Internet Resources
David Leadbetter Golf Academy
www.davidleadbetter.com
ESPN
Information on top players, tournaments, golf courses, etc.
www.espn.go.com

Golf Today
Online golfing magazine with weekly bulletins and golf news.
www.golftoday.co.uk
WorldGolf.com
An online golf publication which lists golf schools around the world.
www.worldgolf.com

Bibliography
Andrisani, John, *Play Golf like Tiger Woods* (HarperCollins)
Dear, Tony, *Good Golf Made Easy* (HarperCollins)
Els, Ernie, with Newell, Steve, *The Complete Short Game* (HarperCollins)
Els, Ernie, with Newell, Steve, *How to Build a Classic Swing* (HarperCollins)
Golf World, *Improve Your Golf* (HarperCollins)
Jacobs, John, with Newell, Steve, *50 Greatest Golf Lessons of the Century* (HarperCollins)
Lawrensen, Derek, *Sunday Telegraph Golf Course Guide* (HarperCollins)
Leadbetter, David, *Faults and Fixes* (HarperCollins)
Leadbetter, David, *The Fundamentals of Hogan* (HarperCollins)
Leadbetter, David, *Golf Swing* (HarperCollins)
Leadbetter, David, with Simmons, Richard, *100% Golf* (HarperCollins)
Leadbetter, David, *Positive Practice* (HarperCollins)
Newell, Steve, *A Round with the Tour Pros* (HarperCollins)
Parr, Sandy, *A Little Book of Golf* (HarperCollins)
Sanderson, Sarah, *Shape up Your Golf* (HarperCollins)
Vickers, Jonathan, *Pocket Golf Rules* (HarperCollins)
www.getmapping.com, *Golf Courses* (HarperCollins)

Index

*Numerals in italics refer to
illustrations*